The Axis of Shame

Great Britain, Israel, the United States, and Turkey in the Middle East

How the Middle East Mess Came About and the Only Possible Solutions

---

BY ARTHUR C. HASIOTIS, PH.D.

DORRANCE PUBLISHING CO., INC.
PITTSBURGH, PENNSYLVANIA 15222

ISBN: 978-1-4349-0682-3

Printed in the United States of America

First Printing

For more information or to order additional books, please contact:
Dorrance Publishing Co., Inc.
701 Smithfield Street
Pittsburgh, Pennsylvania 15222
U.S.A.
1-800-788-7654
www.dorrancebookstore.com

Dedicated to my lifelong friend George S. Theodore, Esq., Boston Latin School classmate and fellow graduate and a faithful confidant.

TABLE OF CONTENTS

This is a view that first describes the Middle East policies of Great Britain and the United States that led up to the attacks of September 11, 2001, and second proposes comprehensive solutions that require major sacrifices from all the major participants in this modern tragedy.

Most citizens of the United States and their friends around the world were astounded by the September 11, 2001 attacks on New York City and Washington, DC. Did the attacks represent the work of madmen, misguided religious zealots, or calculating militants who felt that this was the only practical way to achieve their goals? Do these attacks represent the opening phase of a long Armageddon type of struggle between civilizations and cultures, or a new chapter in the "eternal struggle" between good and evil? Should people study Islamic doctrines and texts for the keys to these events? Can these individuals be stopped and these catastrophic events prevented by military and security measures? Why is the government of the United States hated or, at minimum, viewed with grave suspicion by many individuals in the Arab countries as well as in many other Islamic societies?

CHAPTER I
THE HISTORICAL BACKGROUND

The general Islamic view of the Christian European world was strongly conditioned by events that took place during the seventh through the thirteenth centuries AD. These events witnessed the rapid spread of Islam in the Middle East, North Africa, Central Asia, and later India, and the South Asian archipelago. Europe, except for Spain, remained very resistant to the Islamic tide of conquest. The repeated military successes of the Eastern Roman Empire (also known as the Byzantine or Later Roman Empire centered at Constantinople) in blocking and defeating massive Moslem land and sea invasion attempts of Europe (especially in 677 AD and 717–718 AD) for more than four centuries (the seventh through the eleventh centuries) created a mentality of frustration and hostility on the part of the Moslems toward the "infidel European Christians." The Moslem raids from Spain into France, particularly during the eighth century, were very threatening and disruptive, but were not on the order of massive invasions with the aim of permanently occupying Western Europe. However, had the West European Christians not fiercely resisted these incursions, the Moslems probably would have developed more ambitious invasion plans for Western Europe.

The harsh reality of the Moslem-Christian conflict of these centuries was that the political and military center of gravity of the Islamic movement was in the zone between Damascus and Baghdad, directly confronting the eastern regions of the Roman Empire centered at Constantinople. The defeat of the Eastern

Roman Empire would have eliminated the only serious military impediment to the flooding into Europe of massive Islamic armies and would have dramatically changed forever the nature of an immature European medieval society. The Renaissance as we know it would not have occurred and Arabic would have displaced Greek and Latin as the crucial language of religion and education. One of the religious motivations for the attempts to invade and conquer the Eastern Roman Empire was the Islamic view that Muhammad (the "Prophet") had been contacted as a "messenger of God" to bring the clarified "word of God" as a corrective to the "misinterpretations" (from the Islamic view) in the teachings and writings of those who composed the New Testament as well as the works of other early Christian Church leaders. The capture and conversion to Islam of Constantinople and its empire (the repository and center of European culture and learning and the leading Christian city in the world) would have ensured, in Moslem eyes, the final triumph of Islam over "misguided" Christianity.

In spite of the hostility between East Rome (Constantinople) and the Moslems, there was much contact between these rivals. Islamic civilization became a cultural and intellectual competitor of East Rome and was far advanced compared to Western Europe, which had been overrun by numerous barbarian invaders from Asia and Scandinavia. The Islamic societies of these centuries had adopted their own versions of the classical Greek, Roman, and Hellenistic heritages from the surviving centers of classical and Hellenistic civilization at Antioch, Alexandria, and Constantinople itself. The Moslems added significantly to the body of Western learning and established leading centers of education in the sciences, medicine, mathematics, astronomy, the arts, and philosophy at Baghdad, Cairo, Damascus, and Cordova. Students from Spain, Italy, France, and East Rome studied at these Islamic educational centers. A considerable number of these students converted to Islam, feeling that their home societies were incapable of hosting this knowledge and more advanced way of life.

Even though these classical intellectual and cultural influences from Islamic societies reflected Moslem interpretations of the classics and came through the medium of second- and third-hand translations of the Greek and Latin originals, they aided in raising the level of curiosity about classical learning in certain areas of Western Europe, particularly Florence, Genoa, and Venice. These three city-states, because of their many contacts with the Eastern Roman Empire as well as the Arabs, were in the best position to receive Greek scholars, who, with their original classical manuscripts and thorough knowledge of Greek and Latin, would flee the disintegrating Eastern Roman Empire, especially in the fourteenth and fifteenth centuries.

These refugee scholars appeared in Italy, particularly at the *studio* in Florence, and other budding centers of learning in Europe, and would provide crucial intellectual direction to the emerging West European recovery that has come to be known as the Renaissance. The flight of these scholars to the West was the result of East Rome's relentless social, economic, and military decline and its unfortunate position between the rising power of the West European states and the resurgence of Islamic military and political power under Turkish leadership.

From the seventh through the fifteenth centuries, the Moslems experienced eras of political division, internecine military conflicts, and religious dissension among themselves. As the Later Roman Empire began its serious internal decline in the second half of the eleventh century, the Moslems were suddenly confronted with a new and deadly chapter in the relationship between the Christians and the Moslems. This was the crusading period (the eleventh through the thirteenth centuries), when the emerging nations of Western Europe (Roman Catholic peoples) sent several major invasion forces to recapture the Holy Land and, in particular, Jerusalem, from the Moslems and the new Turkish groups that had recently risen to military prominence in the Middle East. While there is no doubt that many individual crusaders were motivated by genuine virtue and religious zeal, many more crusaders were driven by the desire to seize booty and the lands of foreigners. Most of the crusaders had visions of adventure and military glory against the enemies of Christendom. Unfortunately, the great number of very cruel and savage acts committed by the almost universally primitive and uneducated crusaders, not only against Moslem military personnel, but also against Moslem, Jewish, and Eastern Christian civilians, revealed the barbaric side of the crusades. These shameful acts have given the crusading movements an eternally bad name among virtually all of the peoples of the Middle East. The indigenous inhabitants of the Middle East have never forgotten the images, written records, and popular folklore concerning the tens of thousands of Moslems and Jewish captives crucified by the crusaders along the roads leading to Jerusalem. The ruins of numerous crusader castles throughout the Near East (present-day Turkey, Syria, Lebanon, Palestine, and Israel) are constant reminders of this tragic encounter between Western Christendom and Islam. Considering their horrific behavior, it is no surprise that the crusaders found very few allies in the Near East and, eventually, were soundly defeated in the late twelfth century by Islamic forces led by Salah al-Din (Saladin), who was of Kurdish origin. Saladin, instead of massacring his many Christian captives (as was the crusader and Moslem practice with captives), eventually treated them humanely and taught them the basics of truly chivalrous behavior, ideas that are the foundation of the modern world's codes for the treatment of military captives.

The extreme hostility of the crusaders toward the Moslems had been originally encouraged by the authorities at Constantinople as a way to counter the further spread of Islam. The experiences of the West Europeans with the Moslems in military engagements on land and sea prior to the crusades had already prepared a fertile seedbed for a deep dislike of the Moslems. The Islamic conquests of historic Christian lands, such as Syria, Mesopotamia (Iraq), the Holy Land (Israel and Palestine), Jordan, Egypt, North Africa, and Spain, were viewed by most Christians as aggression against "God's peoples and God's lands." In spite of the fact that there were many instances of cruelties inflicted upon Near Eastern Christians by their Moslem rulers, Islamic governments frequently displayed a level of religious and ethnic tolerance that was not approached until the nineteenth and twentieth centuries in the most democratic societies of the West. Still, it was very unsettling to Christians that Moslem military successes had left the Holy Land, with its many religious shrines that were dear to Christians, in the hands of fundamentally hostile rulers.

For most of the Arabs, who had rapidly converted to Islam, the new religion was a powerful political and military rallying point that enabled the Arab peoples to free themselves from either Roman (Constantinople) or Persian domination and occupation. In the seventh century, Islam took on some of the political aspects that we associate with nineteenth- and twentieth-century "national liberation" or "self-determination" movements from European colonial rule. In the view of many Moslems, these “liberated lands” took on the aura of “sacred Islamic soil” that must never again be allowed to fall into the hands of the “infidel” European colonial powers. The crusades, with their extreme violence and unholy intolerance, were seen by many Moslems as the initial attempts by Europeans to create “alien states” in and reestablish colonial control over the Middle East. Certainly, the twentieth-century interwar British and French mandates in the Middle East, and the post-World War II establishment of the Western-oriented state of Israel, seem to fit neatly into the worst apprehensions that the Arabs and Moslems have had concerning their relations with the West. These intrusions into Moslem-held lands, some of which, during the period of the crusades, still had majority Christian populations, constitute very important aspects of the historical perspectives that frame the Arab-Israeli conflict in the commonly expressed views of a vast number of Middle Easterners, both Moslem and Christian.

An often-neglected chapter in the story of East-West interaction during this period was the very serious alienation that had developed between the West European Christians and the Eastern Orthodox Christians. This estrangement had been developing over the centuries and manifested itself in the forms of commercial rivalries, military conflicts, religious disputes, and pogroms against Italian merchants in Constantinople. This growing enmity culminated in the infamous Fourth Crusade of 1203–1204 AD, which led to a fifty-seven–year Latin (Roman Catholic) occupation of Constantinople. This effectively ended the Eastern Roman Empire as an important power and set the stage for the inevitable Moslem takeover of Constantinople.

The revolting and uncivilized acts of the crusaders during the Venetian-led Fourth Crusade, in which Constantinople (by far the greatest Christian city in the world) was captured during Easter week, made East-West reconciliation impossible. The desecration, sacking, and pillaging of its churches, museums, schools, historic buildings, numerous libraries, and historical antiquities, along with the butchering, torture, and rape of fellow Christians, have never been forgotten in the Near East. The crusaders mindlessly destroyed many artifacts of their own cultural heritage.[1] The alienation was so great that when Constantinople was finally captured by the Ottoman State in 1453, most of the small band of defenders were foreign mercenaries (Italians). The most reliable historical sources indicate that more than half of the besieging Ottoman troops and three of their five commanders were Eastern Christians. The Ottoman policies of religious toleration and promotion on the basis of merit resulted in fewer than seven thousand troops (including the Italians) being available to defend the largely abandoned capital. It also helped that Sultan Mehmed II, who had substantial Greek ancestry, had vowed to oust all vestiges of the "Latins" (the Roman Catholics, especially the Venetians and the Genoese) from all the lands where the Orthodox Christians lived.

Also aiding the alliance between the Moslem Turks and the Orthodox Christians were the policies of the emperors that compromised the Empire's legitimacy in the eyes of its own people. These policies basically sought military aid from the West European states in exchange for subordinating the Eastern Orthodox Church to the authority of the Roman Catholic Pope. The very unpopular and humiliating Council of Florence of 1438–1439 AD, at which the Roman Emperor and the Patriarch of Constantinople acceded to the demands of the Papacy, resulted in the alienation of large numbers of the Orthodox Christian populace. It also resulted in the estrangement of the Grand Duchy of Moscow, which had been Constantinople's only real hope for outside military relief. This ill-conceived and counterproductive attempt to absorb, under duress, the Orthodox Church, combined with the earlier tragic Fourth Crusade and the 1242 AD crusading invasion of the Novgorod region of Russia by the Roman Catholic Teutonic Knights, which Alexander Nevsky and his Russians defeated in the Battle of the Ice, cemented Russia's suspicions of and hostile stance toward the West. This Russian hostility toward Western European aggressiveness would remain a background factor in Moscow's involvements in Balkan and Middle Eastern politics into the twenty-first century. These unfortunate events resulted in Constantinople (modern Istanbul) permanently becoming a part of the Moslem world and in the more than four hundred-year Ottoman occupation of the Balkans, with all the tragic consequences that have manifested themselves there in the last hundred years. Roman Catholic-Eastern Orthodox relations have never fully recovered from these events.

It should now be clear why the crusades were important in driving the Moslems and the Eastern Christians together to see the West as a common enemy. It would be nearly five hundred years before the European powers would have the opportunity to reenter the Middle East and build new relationships with the indigenous inhabitants. Of course, the Moslems and especially the Turkish peoples benefited greatly from the deep division between the Western and Eastern Christians. The Turkish-led Islamic world, tolerantly utilizing the talents of its many Christian and Moslem ethnic groups, would reach its military and political zeniths during the sixteenth and seventeenth centuries. However, the Ottoman Empire soon faced difficult military encounters as Western Europe and Russia rapidly became more powerful and aggressive. From the late seventeenth century to the First World War, Islamic assumptions of superiority over Christian societies were deflated as the Ottoman Empire was subjected to repeated military defeats by European coalitions and by Russia. During this period, the Ottoman authorities were confronted with direct threats and pressures from the West and Russia to accommodate European interests, particularly the economic and strategic concerns of Western European nations, and the strategic, military, and religious interests of Russia. After 1700, having fallen behind in technology, in military matters, and in economic development, the Ottomans, with some success, attempted to play the European countries off against each other.

The decline of the once ethnically and religiously tolerant Ottoman Empire was accompanied by the rise of Turkish nationalism and xenophobia. This trend alienated nearly all of the non-Turkish ethnic groups, including the Greeks, who had been so prominent in Ottoman administrations. This xenophobia was accelerated by the Greek War of Independence (1821–1829 AD), which eventually saw most of the major European states (especially Russia) side with the Greek insurgents. The breakaway of the Greeks led to later rebellions against Turkey by other Christian peoples in the Balkans. The Arab inhabitants of the Ottoman Empire were treated with even more disdain than the Christians by the eighteenth- and nineteenth-century Turkish authorities; thus, there was widespread hatred of the Turks by the Moslem and Christian Arabs. This disaffection between the Arabs and the Turks would, during the First World War, lead to an alliance between various Arab groups seeking independence and the British, with the participation of "Lawrence of Arabia." Turkey's disastrous partnership with the Axis powers in World War I set the stage for what could have been an amicable and progressive era in the relationship between the West European powers and the Arabs as well as other indigenous peoples of the Middle East. What happened during the period encompassing the two World Wars (1914–1945 AD) is the immediate seedbed of the current tragic situation in the Middle East.

CHAPTER II
THE INTERWAR INCUBATOR

The defeat of the Ottoman Empire in the First World War led to the end of Turkey's control over Syria, Trans-Jordan (which included present-day Israel, the West Bank, Gaza, and the Kingdom of Jordan), the Arabian Peninsula, and Mesopotamia (Iraq). The League of Nations authorized a British mandate over Palestine (present-day Israel, the West Bank, and Gaza), Jordan, and Mesopotamia, and a French mandate over Lebanon and Syria. These mandates were supposed to be interim administrative bodies that were to prepare these areas for eventual independence. The Arabs viewed the European-dominated League of Nations as simply an instrument for allowing Britain and France to carve up the Middle East into colonial fiefdoms as London and Paris had done in Africa and East Asia. In the light of the important support that the Arabs had given the British in the fight against Ottoman control of the Middle East, many Arabs felt deeply betrayed by London and the League. Modern Arab suspicions of the West began from this point on.

British rule was established in Trans-Jordan and Mesopotamia and was characterized by the familiar European imperial arrogance and the British sense of superiority in cultural matters and social distinctions. Britain's Middle East possessions were viewed as little more than new way stations in the colonial bureaucracy. The Arabs were viewed as a subject and subordinate people who had an interesting history but were now incapable of running their own affairs in the modern world. The possibilities for serious trouble in this dangerous situation were compounded by the fact that many of the senior British leaders of the first half of the twentieth century were under the influence, in varying degrees, of "Christian Zionism," the belief that it was the ultimate divine will that the Jews return to the biblical lands of Israel, so that the Apocalypse could take place with the "Second Coming of Christ" soon following, along with the conversion of all the Jews to Christianity. While it was true that many Jewish leaders were seeking allies wherever they could be found and often cooperated with groups with whom they did not completely agree, it seems likely that most Jews would have harbored serious reservations about the conversion of the Jews in this Christian Zionist program. However, the Zionists could not afford to be too choosy in finding allies.

Chaim Weizmann, the leading spokesperson for the Jewish Zionists (Jews who wished to create a Jewish homeland and state in Palestine), had masterfully developed cordial ties with British Prime Minister David Lloyd George, Foreign Secretary Arthur Balfour, Prime Minister Ramsay MacDonald, and his son, Malcolm MacDonald, as well as American Jewish leaders such as Justice Louis Brandeis.[2] Many of these British leaders and other prominent politicians in Western Europe believed that the needs of the Jews had to be addressed, since it was widely believed that the Jews had vast economic power throughout the world, were in control of large sections of the media, were behind the Ataturk Revolution in Turkey, were responsible for the destruction of the Tsarist government, and were in control of the Bolshevik Revolution. The Goulds, the Rothschilds, the Warburgs, the Guggenheims, and many other wealthy Jews were often viewed in non-Jewish circles as participants in a worldwide network of influence peddling. Whether one could make a realistic case for this characterization of the wealthy Jews of this era was not the important issue. People in responsible positions in the governments and in the economies of Great Britain, the United States, and continental Europe believed that it was true and acted accordingly. After all, the Rothchilds were commonly viewed as one of the great powers of Europe and the world.

An important chapter in what was to become the modern Palestine drama and the later situation of hostility between the Arabs (and other Moslems) on the one hand and the West on the other hand was the divisive Balfour Declaration of November 9, 1917. This declaration called for the establishment of a "national home" for the Jews. It did not call for a Jewish state or a national state for the Jews. At the same time (1917–1918), the British were involved in assisting the Arab rebellion against the dying Ottoman Empire, in which "Lawrence of Arabia" (Thomas Edward Lawrence) was playing a leading role. During this period, the British had committed themselves to some form of Arab independence once the Turks were defeated. Sir Henry MacMahon, the British High Commissioner in Egypt, was the principal involved in these dealings with the Arabs. In both the Balfour Declaration and the promises of some form of Arab independence, the British were characteristically vague about the exact meanings of these "commitments" to the point that both the Arabs and Jews believed that London favored their respective aspirations in Palestine. The Balfour Declaration, from the start, was very controversial and engendered much hostility and contentious discussion. The British consulted with President Woodrow Wilson on the document before proclaiming it to the world. President Wilson was initially opposed to making the Balfour Declaration public and official. Chaim Weizmann contacted Louis Brandies (one of the most prominent American Jews), who then used his influence to convince Wilson to allow the British to proceed with the proclamation. Many in the British and French governments saw this as proof that the "vast power" of "world Jewry" extended throughout the United States right into the White House.[3] Many British military officers opposed the Balfour Declaration as unrealistic, since at least 90 percent of the population of Palestine was not Jewish, but mainly Arab. An example was Brigadier General Sir Gilbert F. Clayton, who simply believed that attempting such a policy would necessitate an ethnic transformation on a scale that would provoke violent reactions from the Arabs, who were in the vast majority.[4]

The reality of this Arab majority in Palestine was attested to in numerous eighteenth- and nineteenth-century accounts of travelers to the area, as well as Turkish and British government records. The Zionists, at various times, have tried to counter the preceding reality with two incompatible arguments. The first claims that Palestine was largely uninhabited and that the Arabs (Palestinians) were nearly all brought into Palestine as employees and laborers by Jewish settlers. This argument is in conflict with all non-Arab and non-Jewish evidence. In the second argument, some Zionists claim that the

Palestinian Arabs are the descendents of the peoples who occupied the lands of the Jews after the diaspora that followed the Roman-Jewish wars of the first century AD. In this scenario, the Jews of two thousand years later have the right, and in reality, the messianic obligation, to take back these lands in any way possible. This argument sounds like the kind of thinking that is associated with contemporary Arab militants, Moslem extremists, and terrorists. This line of thinking, if adopted by the rest of the world, would have virtually every nation battling its neighbors over lands possessed centuries and millennia ago. Religious and mythological justifications for aggression and killing would abound in a world that would be characterized by irrational hatred and extreme ethnocentrism. This scenario sounds like some of the activities carried out by ultra-nationalists in the 1930s and 1940s. Similar outrageous activities are being played out in the present-day Middle East. The biblical justification for the creation of Jewish settlements in the West Bank is an example of this type of thinking. In any case, the Zionists will have to decide whether the Palestinian Arabs are the descendents of the people who "sacrilegiously" occupied lands that were "given to the Jews by God," or whether the Arabs were "guest workers" brought into a strangely uninhabited Palestine by Jewish settlers. The Zionist propagandists cannot have it both ways.

BRITISH POLICIES IN THE INTERWAR PERIOD

Without question, British policies in Palestine favored the Zionist Commission by allowing it to have a sizeable bureaucratic structure and by allowing the Commission and Chaim Weizmann to have unfriendly British officials transferred out of Palestine. British favoritism toward the Zionist cause was evident in the appointments of Herbert Samuels as High Commissioner in Palestine in 1920, and later of Harry Luke (both Jews). Samuels's pro-Jewish quota system was very helpful to the Zionist plans. In addition, Jews were granted exclusive economic concessions in many areas, including tariffs that were especially helpful to Zionist entrepreneurial activities. The British also allowed the creation of the paramilitary Jewish Legion. The fact that during the British Mandate over Palestine, the number of Jews increased more than tenfold, unmasks any pretense of British evenhandedness.[5] David Lloyd George and Winston Churchill made sure that Jewish immigration was not stopped and even turned a blind eye to Zionist gun smuggling. Jews who wished to immigrate to Palestine usually were processed through the local Zionist organization rather than the British consulate in their native land. This was a clear and serious abdication of responsibility on the part of the British government.

At the same time, the British authorities in Palestine were battling Jewish and some Arab terrorist attacks aimed both at the British and at each other. In the midst of all this turmoil, many points of view about the future of Arab-Jewish relations in Palestine were put forth and discussed by a myriad of community leaders and intellectuals. Some Jews envisaged a kind of autonomous Jewish state under Prince Faisel, who later actually became king of greater Syria, and even later, of Iraq. Some Arabs called for the complete cessation of Jewish immigration into Palestine. On the other hand, many Zionists felt strongly that the slow dispossession of the Arabs of their land that had started in the late nineteenth century must be continued and accelerated until the Jews constituted a majority of the population of Palestine. David Ben-Gurion and other Zionist leaders attempted to camouflage the true nature of the Zionist objective of removing the Arabs from the area of the future Israeli state by talking about the coexistence of two peoples in one land. These dishonest and deceptive attempts to mask the true goal of Zionism were often exposed by Jewish writers and intellectuals. Militant Zionists like Ze'ev Jobotinsky who were honest and clear about the necessity of expelling the Arabs from Palestine were dismissed by the official mainline Zionist leaders as irresponsible hotheads who did not represent anyone except for some misguided extremists. Others in the Zionist camp pointed to the recent population exchanges between Greece and Turkey in the 1920s as possible models to be considered. Even the seemingly benign population transfers that were taking place in parts of occupied Europe in the late 1930s and the early 1940s under German auspices were looked at as examples, until the inhumane, murderous, and genocidal nature of the Hitler regime rendered its policies and actions unacceptable for emulation.

The successful progression of the Zionist plans for Palestine and the complicity of the British authorities led to the ill-conceived and disorganized Arab riots in Hebron in 1929. Some elements of the Arab population of Palestine had become aware of the Zionist plans to remove them from their lands and replace them with "strangers" from Europe and America (Jewish immigrants). Arab confusion and divisions were apparent in that many Arabs hid and protected Jews in Hebron, while Arab activists and leaders demanded that Britain rescind the Balfour Declaration. During the 1930s, the Arabs began attacking the British as well as the Jews in Palestine. After thirty thousand Jews were allowed to enter Palestine in 1933, Arab rage at the British and the Jews reached new heights and the Arabs began a six-month strike. During the strike, the Arabs debilitated their own cause by constantly fighting among themselves, by continuing to sell land to Zionist groups, and by spying for the Zionists for money. The Palestinian Arabs had not developed social organizations that could evolve into governing institutions. Centuries of subjugation by the Ottomans and isolation from European developments, along with the policies of the British mandate, aided in the perpetuation of this unfortunate political retardation. Thus, the development of Arab nationalist political movements was particularly weak in Palestine.

The chief political task of the Zionists during the interwar period was maintaining British complicity in the program to transform Palestine into a Jewish state. Colonel Frederic Kirsch, a high Zionist official, cautioned the Hebrew newspapers to tone down their criticism of the British authorities or risk the loss of British pro-Jewish sympathies. He felt very strongly that the Zionist plans for Palestine could not be realized without continuing British support.[6] Strong Zionist influence over the British politicians of this era is evidenced by the strange demise of all the elaborately prepared and researched "White Papers" that called for the reversal of the British policies of acquiescing to Zionist plans for continued immigration of Jews into Palestine. Another very important reason for the ineffectiveness of all the British "White Papers" was that Zionist terrorists made it known that they would target anyone who strongly advocated any of these documents. The British failure in Palestine reflected London's lack of practical purpose and sensible political vision for the area. London's policies seem to have coalesced around the idea that Britain could establish a stable imperial position for itself by building up the Jews to the point where they would become an effective counterweight to the Arabs, and London could ultimately control things by being indispensable to the Jewish inhabitants of Palestine, who would then become London's surrogates. This approach required continued Jewish immigration into Palestine and, in reality, called for massive Jewish immigration so that the Jews would become the overt rulers of Palestine and the British would become the guarantors of the Zionist enterprise. These unrealistic plans were formulated within the context of a worldview that Zionist forces not only controlled Great Britain, but also the U.S., the USSR, and all the other major countries of Europe and the Americas. Obviously, the British greatly overestimated their ability to manage the Zionists and events in Palestine.

THE BRITISH DILEMMA IN THE 1930S

Increasingly, the British realized that they had worked themselves into a situation in Palestine for which they had no solution. Both the Arab and Jewish militant groups were resorting to terror. During the 1930s, more than two hundred fifty thousand Jewish immigrants, twice the number of the 1920s, had been allowed by the British Mandate authorities to settle in Palestine. Those who claim that Israel was established in spite of British opposition are truly out of touch with reality. It is a fact that many people in Great Britain saw in the idea of a Jewish homeland a chance to correct a "great historic wrong" and, at the same time, work for a goal imbued with biblical overtones. Above all, it appealed to that "British sense of fairness." Apparently there was no place for the Palestinian Arabs in that "British sense of fairness." Not only did the British treat the Palestinian Arabs less fairly, they also treated them more harshly and frequently even quite inhumanely. British actions against Arab terrorists were much more severe than against Zionist terrorists. From 1935 on, Arab homes were routinely destroyed and villages and homes were physically occupied for months. Men and women were searched, interrogated, and indefinitely detained, and families and villages were subjected to collective punishments. Many of these policies have been implemented by the contemporary Israeli authorities against Palestinian Arabs. As terrorism grew, the British authorities placed Arabs in forward vehicles and train cabs as human mine detectors. Jews were never treated in this manner. All these policies were similar to ones used by the British in India. Also, Arab terrorists convicted of murder were usually executed, while Zionists in similar circumstances were almost never executed.

It was apparent that London did not have the courage or the will to tame the Zionist thugs who were running wild in Palestine. The "Night Squads" of Orde Wingate; the Etzel, Palmach, and Lechi (Stern gang), which were the terrorist units of Haganah; the special operations units; and their smaller Arab counterparts, all involved themselves in killings and lootings. In spite of these violent activities, the British authorities increasingly worked closer and closer with the Jewish Agency, which had functioned for many years as a kind of Zionist shadow government in Palestine, with London's acquiescence. Even the 1944 Lechi murder of Lord Moyne, the British senior representative in Egypt, did not derail the continued growth of British-Jewish cooperation. In cases where the British did strike back at Jewish terrorists, such as "Operation Agatha" after World War II, their actions were nothing like the brutalities and cruelties visited upon the Palestinian Arabs by Major General Bernard Montgomery during the anti-Arab campaign of 1938. General Montgomery's career is stained with a large blot from this campaign. Considering the actions of the British in favoring the Zionist cause, Arab overtures to Hitler and the European fascist movements are understandable within the amoral theory of "the enemy of my enemy is my ally." The dangerous nature and unsoundness of this theory in regard to Arab-Nazi relations is evident in that eventually, the Nazi anti-Semitic policies would have led to murderous actions against the Arabs themselves, who are the largest Semitic group in the world.

THE FRUITS OF THE BRITISH MANDATE

While London could point to a variety of infrastructure improvements and the imposition of some elements of basic law and order, the mandate also allowed heavy Jewish immigration into Palestine, stopped meaningful Arab countermeasures, and set the stage for the seemingly insoluble Arab-Israeli conflict that has dominated the Middle East to the present time. After the Second World War, Britain turned its Middle East problem over to the United Nations. London basically abandoned the mess that British policies had permitted to develop in Palestine. London saw no way of handling the Arab wrath that its irresponsible policies had brought into existence. As their final pro-Zionist act before leaving, the British, who had allowed the Zionists to develop political and security organizations, turned over the everyday practical political and security operations in Palestine to the Zionists.[7]

With the historical background of the periodic oppression and brutal killings that the Jews had endured at the hands of virtually every European host country, and the horrors of the largely realized Nazi extermination programs for the Jews, the vision of Chaim Weizmann and other leading Zionists of a permanent European presence (by Jews) in the Middle East was about to be fulfilled in Palestine. Considering the terrible experiences that so many Jews had had in nearly all of their non-Jewish host societies around the world, it should surprise no one that a great number of Jews viewed Palestine as a kind of haven and promised land. Certainly, all the Jews who favor Israel should be thankful to Great Britain for acting as the crucial catalyst in the emergence of Israel. On the other hand, nearly all Arabs despise Great Britain for its central and decisive role in the emergence of Israel.

CHAPTER III
THE POST-WORLD WAR II TRAGEDY

In 1947, the United Nations, under the domination of the victorious Allies, responded to the British admission of failure to resolve the Palestinian situation by relieving London of its mandate over Palestine and by sanctioning a partition of Palestine against strenuous Arab objections. The initial response of the Arab states was to send in military forces to destroy any Zionist fighting units and to occupy the lands given to the Jews under the United Nations partition plan. In reality, the Arab military forces displayed many of the characteristics usually associated with the parade armies of the British and French colonial administrations. These armies had not been trained to fight independently, for that would have made them potential threats to their colonial masters. While some native officers were trained, the Arab armies had been largely trained and commanded by senior and junior grade officers from the colonial mother country. Experienced native officers were the exception. With minor exceptions, the Arabs, even though they possessed air forces (the Israelis initially had no planes), were unprepared for serious military action. Many Arabs who fought in WWII had been demobilized.

In contrast, the Zionist forces, though fewer in number, had the Haganah (Jewish Army) and the Palmach, Irgun, and Lechi (military and paramilitary forces that shaded from regular military units to terrorist gangs). These groups had a wealth of experience gained during the period of British rule and thus were far better prepared than the confident but very inexperienced Arab forces sent against them. A crucial psychological factor that favored the Jews was that if they lost, they really had nowhere to go. They truly had their backs against the wall. The Jewish settlers in Palestine, even though most were refugees from European oppression, represented and reflected the gulf between Europe and the Middle East in terms of technology, tactics, organization, and administration. The superior European-influenced leadership and organization of the Jews were crucial in their success in this first struggle with the Arabs. The Arabs were severely disadvantaged by their relative lack of modernity in many spheres of politics and military matters. In addition, the Arab cause, in this first military struggle with what was for all practical purposes an independent Zionist political and military entity, suffered a critical loss. The death of Sheik Abd al-Kader al-Husseini at Kastel deprived the Palestinians of their only potentially effective leader. Unfortunately, the Sheik's call for the killing of all the Zionists was not in the best tradition of Salah al-Din (Saladin). Also, the murderous Zionist attack (April of 1948) on the Arab village of Deir Yassin, where 110 Arabs (nearly all noncombatants) were killed, became a major propaganda disaster for the Arabs when they falsely claimed that the Zionist forces had committed many atrocities, including rape and outright murder. This misleading propaganda led to the flight of several hundred thousand Arabs from the territory of the future state of Israel. All told, approximately 650,000 Arabs, for numerous reasons, fled from the Zionist-controlled areas of Palestine. Ultimately, most of these refugees found it not possible to return to their homes in the newly proclaimed state of Israel, thus easing the ethnic pressures within Israel. In the final analysis, the Arabs of Palestine were the hapless victims of a calculated and insidious long-term conspiracy by the British and the Zionists to mask their true intentions of bringing to fruition the "manifest destiny" of the Israelites. Dictating this British collusion with the Zionists was what Lloyd George and other British politicians believed to be the wishes of the true power brokers of the world (the "international Jewish money lords"), who could decide the fates of governments in Europe and the Americas. Winston Churchill, a very strong backer of Israel, was known to have depended on largess and loans from prominent Zionist individuals.

During the summer of 1948, David Ben-Gurion announced the establishment of the state of Israel. As in the administration of

President Woodrow Wilson, in regard to the Balfour Declaration, there was strong opposition to the recognition of an Israeli state by the United States. President Truman went against the strong opposition of both General George C. Marshall and the U.S. State Department and ordered the recognition of Israel. General Marshall, the chief architect of the military victories of the western Allies in the European and Far Eastern theaters of World War II, believed that the creation of Israel would lead to endless wars in the Middle East and to the growth of insoluble problems in that area. General Marshall also accused Truman of a transparent attempt to win the "Jewish vote" and the financial backing of powerful Jewish-money interests (that so-called "network of Jewish money lords") for his upcoming presidential reelection campaign. This debate within the Truman administration had been played out prior to the proclamation of the state of Israel, for it was only a few minutes between the proclamation and the announcement of American recognition of Israel at the United Nations. If any American wants to know when serious suspicions and resentment of the U.S. began among the Arabs and many non-Arab Moslems, all one has to do is listen to the words of the delegates of the Islamic countries at that United Nations session. Their comments and written statements are very clear in stating that a grave injustice had been committed against the Palestinian Arabs by the West. The U.S. was the most prominent advocate of recognition, but it was not alone. Great Britain, the USSR, and France quickly followed, and Russia even allowed Czechoslovakia to supply arms to the Israelis.

THE POST-1948 ARAB-ISRAELI WARS

In the aftermath of the first Arab-Israeli war, the Palestinian Arabs were left with nothing in terms of political power. Some remained under Israeli rule, Jordan occupied the West Bank, and Egypt took the Gaza Strip. In 1954, Britain continued its colonial downsizing by abandoning its Suez Canal military bases. In 1955, President Nasser of Egypt turned to the USSR and Czechoslovakia for modern weapons. During this period, both Egypt and Israel were attempting to infiltrate and destabilize each other. General Moshe Dayan and other Israeli leaders, fearful that the Egyptians would become proficient in the use of these modern weapons, urged a preemptive strike against the Nasser regime. An aggressive military stance has been a recurring theme in Israeli military thinking. On July 26, 1956, President Nasser nationalized the Suez Canal. This act brought Britain, France, and Israel together in the ill-fated attempt to reoccupy the Suez Canal zone by military force in October of 1956. Israel invaded Egypt and seized the Sinai Peninsula. Without question, Egypt was the victim of calculated military aggression. To the dismay and shock of Britain, France, and Israel, the United States sided with the USSR at the United Nations and both powers called for the immediate withdrawal of the invading forces. The U.S. was unwilling to condone a blatant neo-colonial adventure. This move was not only in the best foreign policy tradition of the United States, but also deflated and discredited Soviet Bloc propaganda about American imperialism, and made the U.S. appear to be less of a menace to the Arabs and more evenhanded in the Middle East. United Nations troops were placed along the Egyptian-Israeli border.

The 1967 Arab-Israeli War was to some extent a manifestation of Cold War machinations, with the USSR fishing in troubled waters. Many young Arab military leaders, aspiring politicians, and bureaucrats were attracted to the apparent rapid rise of Soviet power through the socialist model of development. With "Arab socialism" as a new and seemingly growing force in the Middle East, Moscow hoped to shift the balance of forces in the region to its favor with little cost or effort. The Russians irresponsibly spread false rumors in Egypt and Syria that Israel was massing troops at the Syrian border.[8] In May of 1967, President Nasser ordered the UN troops patrolling the Egyptian-Israeli border to leave. Because Egypt would now control Sharm El Sheik, Israel was faced with the closing of the shipping route through the Straits of Tiran. Both the U.S. and the USSR admonished their respective allies not to start a war. Later, in May of 1967, the Jordanian Army was placed under Egyptian command.

Israel, exhibiting a high level of recurring strategic paranoia and feeling encircled by heavily armed enemies, initiated the hostilities and struck at airfields in Sinai and the Nile Delta. Jordan lost the West Bank and East Jerusalem. Israel attacked Syria and captured the Golan Heights. At this point, the USSR threatened to send in its own forces, and the U.S. negotiated with Moscow with the aim of bringing about an Arab-Israeli ceasefire. The offers by Israel to return the Sinai Peninsula and the Golan Heights in exchange for peace were unacceptable in the light of Arab military failures and the deep-seated Arab feeling that Israel should not be in the Middle East. There can be no doubt that American military training, modern equipment, and intelligence assistance were important advantages for Israel in this war. These realities only increased Arab anger at the United States and its now obvious policies of favoring Israel in spite of its aggression. President Nasser died in October of 1970 after having unsuccessfully offered to resign in the wake of the 1967 military calamity. The Egyptian public overwhelmingly viewed him as a hero just for having the courage to stand up to the foreign powers. Regardless of his negative aspects, he seems to have manifested a sense of Arab importance and self-worth for many downtrodden Egyptians. The Yom Kippur War of 1973, in which the Arabs were the aggressors, revealed much-improved Arab military forces, but because of Soviet military policies, the Arabs were never brought up to the highest levels of military training and weapons proficiency. These Soviet policies probably reflected Moscow's inability to trust a country that was not under its direct control. In terms of conventional military operations, the Yom Kippur War allowed the Arabs a new and much higher level of military honor and recognition, but in reality, reconfirmed Israel's military superiority.

Since the end of hostilities in 1973, the two most important developments that eventually emerged in the Israeli-Palestinian Arab conflict have been the beginnings of the officially unauthorized Israeli settlements in the West Bank in 1977, under the administration of Prime Minister Menachem Begin, and the rise of the *intifada* and the proliferation of various types of attacks by Arab groups from the Gaza Strip and their spread to East Jerusalem and the rest of the West Bank. Neither side has been willing or able to control these developments. This stalemated situation has continued up through the administrations of Presidents William J. Clinton and George W. Bush. The Obama administration has inherited this very unpromising deadlock.

CHAPTER IV
THE COLD WAR, THE UNITED STATES, AND THE MIDDLE EAST

The Cold War increasingly came to dominate the actions of all the principals in the Middle East situation. The initial appearance of evenhandedness in U.S. policies in regard to the Middle East was to a significant degree the result of the Cold War rivalry not yet having reduced anti-colonialism to a secondary-level position in America's overall foreign policy considerations. Also important was the influence of the U.S. State Department Arab specialists. But as the power of the these Arab specialists declined, the growing lobbying influences and campaign contributions of the American oil industry, the automobile industry, the suburban real estate developers, the highway builders, and the many pro-Israel groups throughout the U.S. and the world intensified and came to dominate U.S. Middle East policies.

The interests of the first four of these lobbying groups required that Middle East petroleum products be available to American and European customers at low prices; otherwise, the economies of the United States and many of its allies would be driven into recession and possibly depression. This necessitated that pre-modern, reactionary, and often corrupt and despotic regimes in the oil-producing Middle Eastern countries be kept in power. Unfortunately, this would come to mean that the U.S., periodically, would have to aid in the suppression of popular and democratic-type opposition movements in some of these Islamic countries. America's willingness to intervene decisively in the internal affairs of Middle Eastern nations manifested itself as early as 1953 in its involvement in the overthrow of the popular though anti-Western Mossadegh government in Iran. This government was hostile to the continued domination of Iran by Western governments and of its oil industry by Western oil companies. This CIA-MI6 success in getting rid of a noncompliant Iranian government would eventually evolve into the disastrous 1979 ouster of the U.S.-backed regime of the Shah, the emergence of a virulently anti-American government, the seizure of the U.S. Embassy by Islamic militants, and the severing of diplomatic ties between Iran and the United States. As of 2010, those diplomatic ties remain severed.

In the 1950s and before, Western control of Middle Eastern oil was considered crucial to both Britain and the United States. Iran had been a very important part of the equation of controlling the price and availability of petroleum. It was after the overthrow of the Mossadegh government that Washington became the major supplier of weapons to Iran and Israel, and later Saudi Arabia. Turkey had been a U.S. arms client since its participation in the Korean War under the auspices of the United Nations. The Western-backed overthrow of the Iranian government in 1953 fit very well into the plans of the many pro-Israel lobbying groups, as well as into the wishes of the international oil companies. The Iranians are not an Arab people or a Semitic people, in contrast to all of Israel's immediate neighbors. Also, the Shah of Iran, possibly because of his dependence on American support to survive, was amenable to more friendly relations with Israel. The physical size of Iran and its large population were viewed by many Israelis and their Western supporters as important counterbalances to Israel's many Arab enemies.

The big international oil companies feared losing their influence over the Iranian oil industry. It was hoped by the West and Israel that Iran, under the Shah, would act as a moderating force among the oil-exporting countries of the Middle East. The policies of the United States in the Middle East increasingly became a balancing of "Big Oil's" interests and the wishes of the pro-Israel lobby groups. America would furnish military equipment, training, and numerous infrastructure improvements to cooperating Middle East oil-exporting countries. The U.S. would also provide military security for those states in exchange for non-belligerence toward Israel and for maintaining reasonable stability in world oil markets. In spite of these arrangements, the oil-exporting countries at times found it virtually impossible not to show hostility toward Israel and its U.S. backer. The Arab frontline states (Egypt, Lebanon, Jordan, and Syria) that abutted Israel were not important oil exporters, and were treated in a less accommodating manner than their oil-exporting neighbors.

With the reality of the emergence of the Cold War, the oil-poor frontline Arab states found the USSR to be their main source of modern arms to counter the Israelis. While Soviet aid was welcomed by many in the frontline states, Russia's historic role as the great opponent of the spread of Islam, its dominant role in the collapse of Ottoman military power, and the USSR's advocacy of atheistic communism made it very difficult for Moscow to find sincere friends in the Middle East. On another level, there appeared to be little chemistry between the mostly cautious and closely supervised Soviet Bloc military advisors, aid specialists, and diplomatic representatives and the usually more outgoing and personable Arabs. As the U.S. became more and more tolerant of questionable Israeli actions (preemptive attacks and harsh and brutal reprisals) in Lebanon and the West Bank, Washington was increasingly seen as, at best, an accomplice to, and at worst, an open backer of what nearly all Arabs viewed as Israeli aggression. Never during this period and right through to the end of the twentieth century did America ever officially call for the establishment of an independent Palestinian Arab state. The Arabs of Palestine, who for over a thousand years had been the majority indigenous inhabitants of what today comprises the territories of Israel, the West Bank, and the Gaza Strip, were not deemed by official U.S. policy to be deserving of their own state. While the Zionists, who began to immigrate in significant numbers into Palestine in the late nineteenth century and the first half of the twentieth century, and used every subterfuge to conceal their true intent, were encouraged and recognized by Washington in their statehood plans. This seeming incongruity may be a result of America's own historical experience of taking land by force from the Native Americans and seeing it part of a larger plan for achieving the "New Jerusalem." This transfer of a continent was accomplished through the possession of superior technology by the Europeans, much as the European Jews possessed superior technology and organization in their taking of lands in Palestine. However, in the case of the conquest of North America, there was no one to stand behind and back up the Native Americans. In the case of the Palestinians, regardless of the fact that they have suffered ill treatment from their coreligionists, there are over two hundred million Arabs and another one billion Moslems who feel that the West and the Israelis have been very unfair in their policies toward the Palestinian Arabs. The cry of the Arabs is for justice and fairness.

The continuing consequences of these unrealistic policies of the British, Israelis, Americans, and their allies are intermittent attacks by Moslem militants, Israeli reprisals, unconvincing American peace efforts (except for the work of President Carter), and serious economic, physical, and psychological damage to both the Palestinian Arabs and the Israelis. One can seriously argue that the Balfour Declaration set in motion forces that have resulted in a calamity for all of the Semitic peoples of the Middle East. In reality, these unleashed forces have caused an insolvable civil war within the Semitic world, with ramifications extending to many other regions. It should be noted that Arthur Balfour and many of his "pro-Zionist" contemporaries in Britain, continental Europe, and America, in spite of their "Christian Zionist" leanings, were not known to be particularly fond of Jews. Many cynically viewed a Zionist state in Palestine as a plausible way of ridding their respective homelands of as many Jews as possible as quickly as possible. It cannot be denied that the contemporary Middle East stalemate is to a very large degree a result of the failure of European nations to resolve their own ingrained anti-Jewish currents and treat the Jews in their midst in a manner consistent with the teachings of their supposed leader, Jesus Christ, who was a practicing Jew and religious teacher. Why should the Arabs have the victims of centuries of Christian abuse foisted upon them by conniving European and American politicians? The paramount question that confronts us all in this bloody quagmire is, What is a practical and long-term solution to a problem that never should have been allowed to develop?

CHAPTER V
THE WIDER RAMIFICATIONS OF THE DISASTROUS MIDDLE EAST SITUATION

On September 11, 2001, the United States experienced terrorist attacks of which few U.S. citizens had any understanding. Most Americans and their supporters overseas truly believed that the country had been attacked without discernable cause. Attempts to find answers in the Koran and the tenets of Islam are about as successful as reading the New Testament to find out what motivates Christian religious fanatics. The George W. Bush Administration immediately stated that the attacks were the work of "evil" individuals who hated freedom and the "American way of life." This explanation sounds eerily similar to the wild rants of extremist Moslem clerics describing their Western opponents. Washington went out of its way to state that the Arab-Israeli conflict was not a key element in the attacks. Thus, the initial and subsequent American responses have included aggressive military actions against Afghanistan and Iraq, neither of which have progressed according to the original plans. Much discussion took place about interdicting the operating funds for terrorists and getting out the message to the Moslem multitudes about how wrong they are to view the U.S. in a negative light. The denial of funds to the terrorists assumes that their funds come through normal traceable channels, and that there is some central control and dispersion of these funds. The reality is that most of the funds are moved through unconventional channels. Furthermore, U.S. policies and the post-September 11 military actions (particularly the Iraq invasion) have ensured a vast growth in the numbers of militant and disaffected young Moslems throughout the Islamic world. It has led to a substantial increase in the number of decentralized and autonomous anti-Western Islamic-oriented terrorist groups.

Once again, American self-righteousness and arrogance toward and ignorance of non-Western societies have resulted in ill-conceived and self-defeating U.S. policies. The propaganda plans to change the hearts and minds of Moslems concerning the United States and the West were initially to be run like advertising campaigns similar to corporate attempts to sell soap, soda, and other consumer goods. The U.S. government was so confident and arrogant that it openly discussed how it would easily reduce the Arabs and Moslems to mindless "supermarket" consumers. This incredibly naive, stupid, and pathetic approach to reversing the negative image of the U.S. in the Middle East only served to insult the Arabs and Moslems. Also, it convinced them that in the view of America, they were simply objects to be manipulated and brainwashed so that Washington and Israel could continue on the path to achieving their respective goals, regardless of what issues the Arabs and other Moslems might feel are important to them.

The main American response to the September 11 attacks has been to defeat and destroy (militarily and physically) the terrorists and their organizations. There has been little serious public discussion by U.S. government agencies about changing our ineffective and disastrous policies regarding the Arab-Israeli conflict and our abysmal standing in the eyes of so many Arabs and Moslems throughout the world. American tough-guy talk like "dead or alive" and "bring them on" may go over well on American television, in domestic movie theaters, and among uninformed and blindly patriotic citizens who are looking for simple answers to bedeviling and complex problems, but it seriously damages the interests of the U.S. If Washington does not have the courage to confront the major role that its own foreign policy mistakes have had in aiding and perpetuating these terrorist movements over a period of many years, then America plays into the hands of their militant leaders and assures these extremist movements a growing supply of new recruits.

So how can the United States reverse this increasingly hostile situation? The first lines of defense for any country are its foreign policies. The September 11 attacks took place because over a long period of time, many of America's foreign policies have not only deeply offended many Moslems, but have also been in serious conflict with the much-admired principles that peoples throughout the world (including Moslems) associated with the United States. Some of these principles, such as human dignity, the right of self-determination, freedom from oppression, and liberty and equality for all, are what made the U.S. so attractive to the rest of the world. However, because the U.S. has rarely implemented policies in the Middle East that embodied these highly admired principles, many in the Moslem countries view the U.S. as a hypocritical power that attempts to camouflage its more base objectives behind a screen of high-sounding talk. In other words, many Moslems see the United States as a "phony best hope of the world" that, in reality, seeks to substitute its economic domination for the physical occupation and political domination of the earlier European imperial countries.

The attacks of September 11 were not the first overt acts of a deadly confrontation that is still being played out around the world. In Lebanon, nearly three hundred U.S. Marines were slaughtered in their hotel barracks in 1983 by a terrorist truck bombing. The obtuseness of the American military in lodging these Marines in one multi-story building violated the most basic concepts of military security and dispersion. Of course, the U.S. government and Defense Department foolishly and thoughtlessly viewed these Marines as peacekeepers and not as latter-day "crusaders," which was how they were seen by many Moslems in the Middle East. The first direct major foreign terrorist attack on American soil was the first World Trade Center attack of 1993. The attacks on the U.S.S. Cole and the U.S. embassies in Africa followed. The significance of these attacks was not taken seriously by many U.S. citizens and political leaders, who, because of their lack of historical knowledge, could not make the connections between these anti-American acts and the U.S. policies that have been deeply offensive to many Moslems for decades. The tragically uninformed Americans did not catch the message of all these attacks, September 11 included. That message was that history was not dead, but was very much alive in these attacks on America's homeland, its warships, and its overseas embassies. Washington had been aware of al Qaeda and other terrorist groups for more than a decade before the September 11 attacks. However, in the atmosphere of historical ignorance and self-delusional "superpower arrogance" that pervaded the upper levels of American politics, it was believed by far too many that the U.S. was, for all practical purposes, immune to catastrophic or even serious attacks from terrorist groups. In the naive and fairy-tale mentality that characterized the "Magic Kingdom" of post-Cold War Washington, the few warning voices that did sound alarms were ignored to the peril of the nation.

The basic reason that U.S. foreign policies are viewed as arrogant and are deeply offensive to many people around the world (not just in the Middle East) is that these policy decisions are very frequently not governed by admired American principles, but instead by the interests of lobbying groups that fund the political campaigns of our presidents, senators, congressmen, and governors. America makes fine pronouncements but usually acts in the interests of the farm lobby, the high-technology lobby, the forest products lobby, the organized labor lobby, the petroleum lobby, the pro-Israel lobby, the pro-Turkish lobby, the military-industrial lobby, the real estate lobby, the health-care lobby, the insurance lobby, the professional sports lobby, and many other domestic and foreign lobby groups that have been able to make their views irresistible through their large financial assistance to campaign coffers, particularly on the federal and state levels. While every legitimate and lawful group should have the right and opportunity to be heard by and to lobby our "elected" officials, should we have a political system that places our "elected" officials under intense pressure to vote in certain ways or lose vital campaign funding from certain very wealthy groups or industries? Does the U.S. have truly "elected" officials, or does it have campaigns narrowed down to a few candidates who can attract major funding from powerful lobbies? Does America have a "bought" government that owes its being in office to a circle of determined lobbies? Does the U.S. have democratically elected representatives of the people, or does it have "political opportunists" who represent the interests of their wealthy backers while they give lip service to the concerns of the citizenry? In reality, Washington, DC, including the executive and the legislative branches of the federal government, is the largest and most comprehensive "political auction house" on Earth. Is this one of the major reasons that nearly 50 percent of America's eligible voters do not bother to vote? Why should they bother to vote? It really makes little difference in the

U.S., since big money wins nearly all the time.

Periodically throughout America's history, the democratic process has been corrupted by the extravagant use of money in political campaigns. There are other methods for corrupting politics besides money. These include ballot box stuffing, denial of registration, miscounting and destruction of ballots, multiple votes by certain individuals, and votes cast in the names of deceased persons. Unfortunately, during the second half of the twentieth century, the electoral process underwent a drastic transformation in regard to the funding of campaigns. Traditionally, presidential, senatorial, congressional, and gubernatorial electoral contests have relied upon the political parties as the main conduits for fundraising from the public, with the fundraising efforts of the individual candidates further swelling the amounts available for campaign spending. Since the advent of expensive television campaign advertising in the 1960s, it has increasingly become a race to raise larger and larger amounts of money to overwhelm one's political opponent by means of this very effective medium. Either the candidates, who had become increasingly dependent on lobbying groups for campaign funds, heeded the wishes of these lobbyists, or the money would go to a political rival, whether it be in the current election or in a future election. This is the major reason why the federal and state governments in the U.S. have largely become the servants of the interests of powerful lobbying organizations. This massive American political failure will be corrected only when the president, members of Congress, and the governors are elected through a system of publicly funded campaigns that allow the candidates to be free of raising money. This will enable them to concentrate on the issues confronting the nation. This is the only way that the power of the special interests will be weakened. Also, it will eliminate the power of these lobbies to determine how far a candidate will be able to progress in the electoral process. Our politicians should not be spending huge amounts of time trying to raise oceans of money to stay in office. Our elected officials should be spending their time tending to their political and legislative tasks. Publicly funded political campaigns would make our elected officials more independent and thus more capable of resisting the pressures of the affluent lobbyists. Many questionable spending programs that benefit the groups represented by the lobbyists could be looked at realistically, and ultimately, the people's tax dollars would not be easily used for the selfish purposes of these wealthy interests. America's lobby-dominated government and its inability to view Middle East problems objectively contributed mightily to the attacks on the U.S. and the launching of our foolish and tragic adventure in Iraq.

In view of the preceding discussion of the corrupt U.S. political system, it is not surprising that Washington reacted to the September 11 attacks with denunciations of an "axis of evil" that must be met with stern military responses. President Bush called for elaborate domestic and foreign security measures and the establishment of a powerful new cabinet post of "Homeland Security." Domestic security has been bolstered by giving more powers to the FBI, the attorney general, and the local police. The administration has used every argument possible to expand the power of the executive branch and diminish the legal safeguards written into the Constitution to protect the rights of citizens and aliens in the United States. A golden opportunity to demonstrate to the world that America represented a higher and more civilized standard of behavior was completely lost by the Bush administration's handling of the prisoner issues and its insistence on not following international guidelines from the Geneva Conventions on the treatment of foreign combatants. Their sick attempts to deny that the U.S. was employing torture techniques or shipping prisoners to venues where torture was known to be allowed cast the United States in the images of Syria and Turkey.

The president and the Congress made little effort to call for a serious and open discussion of why the United States was so unprepared for the attacks and what was central to igniting the September 11 attacks upon America. Our "elected" ("bought") leaders would not or could not call for a major rethinking of our failed and shameful foreign policies in the Middle East. It is not in the interests of the petroleum lobby and the various pro-Israel lobbies to have an open and honest discussion of why these policies have led us to our current Middle East dilemma. These policies are aggressive and invasive and have fostered the steady escalation of Western influences into Islamic societies that have deep-seated historic antipathies toward the West. At the same time, many citizens of these traditional Moslem societies are drawn to some Western ideas and material goods. This situation has created severe social and political stresses in many Islamic countries. Furthermore, American policies have worked to deny the Palestinian

Arabs the basic right of self-determination and an independent status, free from subjugation and continuing humiliation at the hands of the U.S.-armed, -trained, and -backed Israelis. In spite of all this, the United States has the gall to claim that it is acting as an "honest broker" and in an evenhanded manner. Only President Carter can claim the role of a friend to all sides.

At least the Israelis were being honest at Camp David in 2000 when they revealed their best offer to the Palestinian Arabs, even though to any nonpartisan observer, the Israeli plan appeared to be disrespectful and shameful. It was a combination of South African apartheid-inspired *bantustans* and nineteenth-century American Indian reservations. The precarious security, military, and territorial situations of Israel make it impossible for Israel to act in a fair and moral manner in its negotiations with the Palestinian Arabs. Israel's often seemingly unfair and brutish actions in regard to its relations with the Arabs are the result of Israel also being a victim of absurd British policies that allowed Israel to emerge into an impractical and hostile environment. There is no solution to the Arab-Israeli disaster until that environment undergoes major changes. These major changes will require far-reaching concessions by all the principal parties, including the United States and Britain.

The United States has an unfortunate parallel policy of favoring the Turkish authorities in regard to the subjugation of the large Kurdish population of southeastern Turkey. For decades, in defiance of the United Nations and many European governments, Turkey denied that the Kurds were even a separate ethnic or cultural group, and insisted that the Kurds were actually "Mountain Turks." The Turkish government, under very strong pressures from the European Union—but not the United States—recently allowed limited use of the Kurdish language in business transactions, in schools, and in radio and television broadcasts. These concessions by Ankara were made in hopes of aiding the Turkish candidacy for membership in the European Union. The United States has shamefully attempted to convince the EU to admit Turkey without any meaningful reforms in Ankara's scandalous treatment of the Kurds. Thankfully, the European Union, unlike the United States, has shown real moral fortitude and courage in rejecting these outrageous American attempts to whitewash Turkey's bloodstained record in regard to the Kurdish people. The brave Kurdish resistance against the brutal policies of suppression by the American-armed and -trained Turkish military has resulted in a decades-long war that has been largely and suspiciously underreported in the U.S. Nearly 40,000 people (mostly Kurds) have been killed and approximately 3,500 Kurdish villages have been destroyed, and their inhabitants have been placed into "detention" camps or "relocated." Both the EU and the UN have repeatedly condemned Turkish atrocities against the Kurds, only to find the "great defender" of human rights, self-determination, and democratic values and procedures, the United States, actively pressuring against and blocking the EU and the UN from putting sanctions on the respective Turkish governments that were guilty of atrocities against the Kurds.

Even more disgraceful, the United States, acting as the handmaiden of an outlaw Turkish repressive regime, went out of its way to aid significantly in the capture of the Kurdish leader Abdullah Ocalen. This hideous American action is roughly comparable to Canadians capturing George Washington (whom London had branded as a terrorist and upon whose head the British had placed a substantial price) and handing him over to London. A more recent example would be the Yugoslav Chetnik nationalist resistance movement assisting the Nazis in the capture of Tito so that he would be executed. If the U.S. found it intolerable to allow the Milosevic regime to commit atrocities in Bosnia and Kosovo, why did Washington fail to intervene in some form in Turkey, supposedly an upstanding member of NATO? The United States, which dominates NATO, apparently tolerates a double standard amongst NATO members that allows Turkey to commit atrocities and genocide. Should not the Turkish political leaders and military commanders involved in these terrible acts be brought to the International Criminal Court in The Hague to be tried for "crimes against humanity"? In collaborating (U.S. military equipment, training, and diplomatic support to Ankara) in the suppression of the legitimate aspirations of the Kurdish people in Turkey, the United States has become a party to Turkey's atrocities and genocidal policies, and has made a mockery of what the NATO alliance claims to stand for. Certainly, Turkey's actions against the Kurds find echoes in the U.S.'s treatment of the Native Americans. In light of America's shameful silence in regard to the Kurds in Turkey, it is not difficult to understand why the U.S. is unwilling to allow itself and its leaders to be subjected to the authority and judgment of the Criminal Court in The Hague in the areas of political and human rights crimes. American involvement in the overthrow of the Iranian government in 1953, the attempts to assassinate Fidel Castro, the policies of regime change in Latin America, the use of chemical agents and carpet bombing in Vietnam, and the irrational and unprovoked invasion of Iraq in 2003 would very likely result in quite a few American leaders being convicted and incarcerated for many years. Can America allow its own criminal acts to go unpunished while it makes judgments of right and wrong on other countries?

In the Middle East, America's policies have degenerated into backing two bullies (Israel and Turkey), both heavily armed and broadly supported by the U.S. While Israel's human rights record is fine for Israeli Jews, it is much less acceptable for the Arab citizens of Israel. To a significant degree, this is an unfortunate result of Israel's unrealistic territorial and precarious military situations. For Israel to have a secure future, it is necessary to make Israel a less-than-attractive place for Arabs, lest, in the future, the Israeli Arabs outnumber the Jews in Israel itself. Turkey's human rights record for ethnic Turks is unacceptable to the EU for well-known reasons. Widespread use of torture by the Turkish police and military, in addition to restrictions on free speech, have been documented by many human rights organizations. Yet these facts have not stopped the U.S. from strongly pressuring Brussels to accept quickly into the EU such an unsuitable candidate as Turkey. Apparently, America feels that Ankara's shameful treatment of the Turkish and Kurdish peoples should not be an impediment to Ankara's admission into an EU that is built upon upholding human rights and requiring civilian control of the military.

Turkey's human rights record in regard to its minority ethnic groups, with the singular exception of the Jews, is one of the worst of any country in the last three hundred years. The savage repression of the Armenians during the eighteenth, nineteenth, and twentieth centuries has been historically documented beyond challenge. The suppression of the Kurds in modern Turkey began in the early years of the Kemalist regime and has reappeared periodically to the present day. The U.S. looked the other way during the unprovoked Turkish government-orchestrated 1953 Istanbul riots against the Greek minority, which destroyed many remaining Christian holdings in Istanbul. The odious American performance over more than thirty years in the Cyprus situation fully reveals that the "best hope for the world" (the United States) is either unwilling or unable to stand up for the rights of either the Greek or the Turkish Cypriots. Certainly, if the population of Cyprus had been 80 percent Turkish and 20 percent Greek, the U.S. government would have had no problem with a Turkish annexation of Cyprus. Unfortunately, the reverse was true, and the hypocrisy of American policies in the eastern Mediterranean was made clear. Because of U.S. backing for the Papadopoulos junta and the U.S. actions in the Cyprus situation, the image of the U.S. in Greece has recovered only partially. Because America has run interference for and favored the post-World War II Turkish regimes, it has been tarnished by its own actions as well as by the uncivilized actions of various Turkish governments. Excuses that Turkey is a special case and must be held to a lower standard because the U.S. needs Turkish military bases were clearly discredited by the initial success of the 2003 invasion of Iraq, which was completed without major Turkish cooperation.

The failings of America's dishonorable policies of favoring Turkey have been apparent for years in Washington's cowardly refusal to bring Turkey to confront truthfully the historically verified Turkish atrocities against the minority Armenian population in 1915 and in earlier times. The archives of Imperial Germany (Turkey's World War I ally), the files of the U.S. State Department, the *New York Times* and other newspapers of record, private eyewitness accounts, and the records of the Turkish government of those times all give irrefutable and reinforcing evidence of these barbaric Turkish genocidal policies toward the Armenian people. Yet even during the Clinton and Bush Administrations, the United States failed miserably to muster the courage, moral fortitude, honesty, and decency to join the European Union and the United Nations in exposing the endless lies of America's Turkish ally. The refusal of the U.S. to recognize the reality of these heinous acts of Turkish governments brands America as a great hypocrite in the Middle East, where the memory of these historic events is very real. The shameful silence of Israeli governments in regard to Turkey's record of atrocities against the Armenians and the Kurds is in line with the disgraceful moral cover-ups that characterize the policies of the members of the "Axis of Shame." After all, Israel, that beacon of democracy and modern Western civilization in the

Middle East, entered into serious military and economic arrangements with apartheid South Africa (disregarding any sanctions) and later with the bogus semi-democratic governments in Turkey.

In its self-appointed role as "moral leader" and "best hope for the world," the United States required that Germany and Italy confront Nazi and Fascist atrocities. Russia and the Ukraine, of their own volition, have investigated and acknowledged Soviet-era barbarities and crimes. Even Austria, Poland, France, and other European nations have honestly admitted that their governments and their citizens were involved in reprehensible and inexcusable events that occurred in their countries. The United States has confronted and acknowledged its inhumane and, at times, genocidal policies toward the Native Americans, its policies of enslavement, disenfranchisement, and peonage toward blacks, and, at various times, movements of rampant discrimination against the Irish, Italians, Jews, Chinese, Japanese, and many other immigrant groups. After some prodding, even Japan has moved, with some backsliding, toward acknowledging its arrogant and barbaric behavior toward subject peoples in Korea, China, and southeast Asia during the first half of the twentieth century and WWII. So why should Turkey, with one of the worst records of human rights abuses, be given a free pass and be the great exception to confronting its own sordid history? Washington, the world is waiting for your explanation of America's disgraceful and shameful actions in support of the various Turkish regimes that have been involved in very serious human rights crimes. Or will the U.S. continue to strive to prove Adolf Hitler correct when he asked, "Who remembers the Armenian massacres?" American policies toward Turkey can only be seen as attempts to consign Ankara's crimes against the Kurds to the invisible and anonymous fate that the U.S. policymakers apparently have reserved for the Armenian massacres. These American policies in regard to Turkey's historic and contemporary human rights violations ooze hypocrisy and show a side of America that allows power and expediency to trample on the high-sounding principles that, at one time, made the U.S. the "hope of the world."

HOW THE UNITED STATES USES ITS BULLIES

Israel's role includes keeping Syria, Jordan, Lebanon, and Egypt confronted and distracted. Egypt is widely viewed in the Middle East as just another U.S. client state that has been bought off with American aid programs and grants so that it will not make any trouble in the area. President Mubarak runs a very effective police state that owes its origins to the period of Egypt's alliance with the USSR. Since these countries have little oil, and with the exception of Egypt's very fine cotton, have not much to export to the West, Israel and the U.S. can treat them with relative indifference. Syria is ultimately under the threat of Turkey's greatly inflated American-supplied and -trained military forces from the north and Israel's technologically advanced military forces from the south. Jordan is connected to the U.S. money line to keep it from straying too far.

Turkey provides America and NATO with staging areas and bases for military deployments in the Middle East and South Asia. This role for Turkey has become more complicated with the electoral success of the pro-Islamic Justice and Development Party and its establishment of a new government. This new party has not been viewed kindly by the U.S. because it is not controlled by the political and military cliques that have normally dominated the parliament, the Grand Council in Ankara, and most post-World War II governments in Turkey. Another "vital" role for Turkey in the eyes of America includes retaining control over the headwaters of the Tigris and Euphrates Rivers, which are situated in southeastern Turkey. Such continued control of these headwaters by Turkey necessitates that all Kurdish independence movements be suppressed. The ability to intimidate Iraq and Syria through the control of this fresh water supply takes precedence over the human rights and dignity of the Kurds. Apparently, in the policies and actions of the country that likes to portray itself as the "land of the free and home of the brave," it is acceptable to have our Turkish "ally" brutally deny freedom, liberty, dignity, and basic human rights to the Kurdish people of Turkey. The Kurds of Turkey, like the Palestinian Arabs, have been treated by the members of the "Axis of Shame" as troublesome pests who deserve little consideration.

The United States, as leader of the "Axis of Shame," in cooperation with military circles in Ankara, has been chiefly responsible for the gross over-militarization of Turkey. If Turkey had a military establishment of normal size for a country of its population and geographic area (approximately half its current military forces), it would be possible to make major progress in raising the living standards and expanding the economic opportunities for the citizens of Turkey. The citizens of Turkey are the victims of American policies that feed the hunger for power of small cliques of Turkish political and military leaders, who traditionally have sat in the Grand Council in Ankara, and until the 2002 election, effectively controlled the actions of Turkey's bogus "semi-democratic" regimes. The recent reelection of the Justice and Development Party with an even greater majority in parliament reaffirms the average citizen's desire for meaningful improvement in living standards and for an end to rampant corruption and police atrocities against the public. The fact that this pro-Islamic Turkish government is less amenable to the desires of the U.S. is a rebuke to Washington's opportunistic and discredited policies of using Turkey for American ends. The recent arrests of militant nationalist conspirators and some retired military officers for allegedly plotting to overthrow the government of Turkey and their being placed on trial gives us hope that the power of America's traditional reactionary allies in Turkish domestic politics may be significantly diminishing.

CHAPTER VI
AMERICAN POLICIES IN THE MIDDLE EAST

The United States needs realistic policies that embody the best values in America's heritage. These are the values of fairness, forthrightness, human dignity, honesty, and respect for the right of self-determination for major national groups. It was these values that attracted people from the Middle East and from around the world to view the U.S. as a different kind of great power from the empires of the past that grossly took advantage of other countries and treated their people in exploitive ways. American foreign policy in the Middle East initially asserted itself strongly in what appeared to be a significant victory. This was the CIA-MI6–assisted overthrow of the anti-Western Mossadegh government in 1953 in Iran. This successful imposition of the Shah regime (a government friendly to the West and Israel) planted the seeds of what would later emerge in 1979 as the virulently anti-Western Islamic Republic of Iran. The emergence of this anti-Western regime meant that the U.S. and the UK lost control of Iranian oil and also of important observation posts into the then-Soviet Central Asian area. U.S. foreign policies and Israel suffered further defeats in that Israel, which had had friendly relations with the regime of the Shah, now was confronted with a very hostile Iranian government.

The lesson here is that regime change by means of diplomatic intrigue or the use of military forces or both is not justifiable unless the target country has embarked upon large-scale aggression against its neighbors or some domestic ethnic, religious, or racial group. However, rather than learn from the Iranian events and consider important changes in its Middle East policies, the U.S. intensified its hostile relations with Iran by supplying and backing the Saddam Hussein regime in Iraq in its war with Iran. Iraq was in the process of loosening its ties with the USSR. The U.S. saw this turn of events as its gain and Moscow's loss. Some time prior to this Moscow had come to the conclusion that Saddam Hussein was unreliable and uncontrollable. The Soviet analysis of Saddam was, in time, to be proven correct, but in the meantime, the U.S. foolishly arranged for Saddam to receive advanced weapons, dangerous chemicals, and deadly biological agents to bolster his military forces in their war with the Islamic Republic of Iran. It was another replay of the very dangerous "enemy of my enemy is my ally" scenario.

This very risky foreign policy axiom was also put into use in Afghanistan, where in the 1980s, the USSR, against the advice of many in its own intelligence agencies, had brainlessly become involved in a spreading and chaotic factional civil war. Seeing themselves as the great anti-communist force and seeking revenge for the U.S.'s humiliating withdrawal from Vietnam at the hands of the Soviet-backed North Vietnamese, elements of the United States government allowed Rep. Charlie Wilson, Dr. Zbigniew Brzezinski, and their congressional and CIA allies to bring about the secret large-scale training and arming of many Afghan and foreign Moslem resistance fighters. Apparently, neither Rep. Wilson nor Dr. Brzezinski was aware of the danger that the "enemies of our enemy" might ultimately be our far more deadly enemies and were using the United States for their own ulterior purposes. Both of these "Cold War warriors" have taken credit quite openly for planning and significantly aiding in the success of the Afghan anti-Soviet resistance movement, but neither has been willing to take responsibility for also being very helpful to the further rise of Moslem militants and fanatics, who, among other things, were emboldened to strike at U.S. warships, embassies, and sites on the U.S. mainland. Even when the Moslem fighters in Afghanistan were receiving vital aid from the U.S., it was no secret that among Moslems in the Middle East, America was viewed as a great enemy of Islamic peoples in that it was the main prop for reactionary Arab regimes and was actively backing and arming Israel.

Furthermore, in their ill-conceived attempt to entrap the "hated" Russians and avenge America's humiliation in its senseless Vietnam adventure, Dr. Brzezinski, Rep. Wilson, and their cohorts managed to become the greatest dupes of America's most deadly enemies (the Islamic terrorists), who indirectly used their help to profoundly humiliate the country that claims to be the only remaining "superpower": the U.S. Among the apparent beneficiaries of the largess of Rep. Wilson, Dr. Brzezinski, and their collaborators were groups both directly and loosely associated with Osama bin Laden and many other Islamic groups deeply hostile to Western ideas and culture. The other beneficiary of U.S. meddling in Afghanistan appears to be, of all people, the Russians, who found in all of this an excuse to "cut and run" out of Afghanistan well before becoming as hopelessly involved as the U.S. did in Vietnam and later in Iraq and Afghanistan. So much for the cleverness of America's Cold War victory in Afghanistan.

THE NEGATIVE IMAGE OF THE UNITED STATES IN THE MIDDLE EAST

During the last sixty-two years, many of the political and military policies and actions of the U.S. in the Middle East have created increasing mistrust of and hatred for America by Moslems. In fact, more and more Moslems see the U.S. as having dethroned Russia as their main foreign enemy. Russia had held this unique position for nearly five hundred years, ever since Tsar Ivan IV (the Sinister) had ordered the storming and capture of the very powerful Khanate of Kazan in 1552. Russia also played the key role in repeatedly defeating Turkey in wars extending across the eighteenth and nineteenth centuries. In spite of public pronouncements blaming "evil people" for the September 11 attacks, the American government recognizes that its image before the more than one billion Moslems is in need of serious improvement. However, changing a country's image as seen by foreigners is a very complicated, difficult, and slow process. The initial inclination of the post-September 11 Bush Administration was to bring in advertising industry executives to sell America to the Moslems. This was abandoned and replaced by films portraying the happy and tolerant lives that Moslems have experienced living in America. These films were oddly reminiscent of pathetic Soviet propaganda films that sought unsuccessfully to convince the world of the cheery and happy lives of Soviet workers and farmers under communism. Neither the Soviet nor the American efforts with such ridiculous and childish propaganda films achieved anything but derision and disbelief from the intended audiences. The clumsy and ignorant character of these infantile attempts to improve the image of the U.S. in the Islamic world revealed that the American government had little understanding of the depths of the problems that it faced. Americans by nature are an optimistic people, who feel there is usually a practical and speedy way to resolve a problem situation. Normally, a combination of bargaining, the spreading around of benefits, and the strategic application of pressure on the right individuals will bring acceptable results. This is an approach that frequently works when everyone involved is mentally concentrating on the immediate contemporary issues. When the situation involves non-European peoples who are deeply conscious of cultural, religious, and military conflicts with Western countries over many hundreds of years, the idea of a quick and relatively painless fix for problems is probably unrealistic.

The Arabs of the Middle East, and in particular the Palestinians, have endured the harsh rule of foreign conquerors. While it is generally accepted that the Assyrian Empire, with its policies of population transfers, created the mixture that became the Arab peoples, their harsh methods of rule were hated by nearly everyone. Next came the Persians, then Alexander the Great with his Greek armies, followed by the Hellenistic kingdoms of Alexander's leading generals, and finally Roman rule, first from Rome and then from Constantinople, for more than seven hundred years. Under the guidance of the new Islamic religion, there was a period of approximately three hundred years of "national liberation" from foreign rule. After the "crusader interlude" (the eleventh through thirteenth centuries), there were a couple of centuries of disunity before the imposition of Ottoman rule that lasted until the early twentieth century, when the West began to foist Zionist rule onto most of Palestine. With this historical record, the Arabs, both Moslem and Christian, have very strong reasons to be highly suspicious of the West.

Another major problem concerning how the many Moslem and particularly Arab countries perceive the U.S., and one that is considered unsuitable for discussion, is the increasing influence of American Jewish groups in the U.S. State Department, the U.S. Defense Department, and the U.S. executive and legislative branches of government. This influence manifests itself not only through the traditional avenues of lobbying politicians and the power of campaign contributions, but also through the presence of a significant number of Americans of Jewish background in the executive and legislative branches of government who at some time have worked as lobbyists for Israel and pro-Israel groups. While this situation is legal under U.S. laws, few Arabs or Moslems can view the U.S. as fair or even-handed under such circumstances. Certainly, if the situation were reversed, and the U.S. executive and legislative branches of government were similarly influenced by Arab-Americans, would Israel and its backers feel that their side could receive a fair hearing or a fair deal from the United States? Let's face it: if Arab-Americans had played the same role in the U.S. government that American Jews have, Israel would not have enjoyed the favored status in the formulation of U.S. foreign policies that it has had since the end of World War II. The fact that Israel is a creature of twentieth-century British and American machinations in the Middle East is what rankles and insults so many Arabs and Moslems. It is most unlikely that the Middle East would be a cauldron of tension and potential war if Britain and the U.S. had not acted to allow the emergence and survival of Israel. From the Arab and Moslem points of view, Israel came into being through the connivance and the surreptitious and ultimately open support of Britain and the United States. The Arabs see the emergence of Israel as being at the root of a great deal of the suffering and problems of the Middle East. These problems will not be solved by clever advertising campaigns or by absurd claims by American politicians that the emergence and continued existence of Israel is not a major factor and a prime spark plug in the ongoing tragic Middle East situation.

CHAPTER VII
THE SOLUTION WILL BE DIFFICULT FOR ALL PARTIES

Palestine is a very small place. Palestine should be one political entity. There is no "two-state solution." Israel came into being by means of what the author Arthur Koestler described as the absurdity of "one nation [Britain] promising to another nation [the Jews] the land of a third nation [the Palestinians]."[9] The creation and survival, through Western machinations, of the state of Israel has brought about the unending chaos and despair of which General George Marshall warned President Truman in the late 1940s. Presidents Wilson and Truman and numerous British leaders have been proven wrong in their Middle East policies in regard to the practicality of the creation of a secure and peaceful Israeli state. If the Palestinian Arabs are allowed to arm themselves with modern weapons, the protrusions of the West Bank and the Gaza Strip into Israel make Israel indefensible. Israel cannot allow the Palestinian Arabs to possess modern tanks, fighter aircraft, and short-range missiles. The "two-state solution" can only mean an Arab West Bank and Gaza Strip that are dependent on and subservient to Israel. The "two-state solution" may seem to Americans a neat and convenient way to resolve a thorny problem, but it will not work unless one believes that it is possible to erect permanent American-style Indian reservations in the Middle East.

The Oslo Accords of 1993 and the Camp David Summit of 2000, regardless of Israeli and American attempts to misrepresent the proceedings, embarrassingly revealed either the unwillingness or the inability—or both—of Israel and its U.S. backer to treat the

Palestinian Arabs as anything but a defeated and dispossessed people who deserved only the minimum in rights and consideration. The establishment of the "Palestinian Authority" in the West Bank by the Oslo Accords was ominously reminiscent of the American government's recognition of the "authority" of Native American Indian chieftains in the nineteenth century. As in the shameful nineteenth-century treaties between the U.S. government and the Native American tribes, the Oslo Accords either avoided the crucial issues or referred to them in vague terms. The "Palestinian Authority's" actual control never extended to more than 35 percent of the West Bank. Israeli Prime Minister Yitzhak Rabin's assassination delayed any further discussion of serious issues until the Camp David Summit of 2000.

American and pro-Israeli spokespersons, including former President William J. Clinton, have constantly claimed that the Camp David Summit of 2000 offered the Palestinian Arabs the best deal that they could ever hope for in that it met virtually all their basic demands. This claim has to be one of the most arrogant insults hurled from one side to the other in a negotiating setting. If one reads the protocols put forth by the Israelis and backed by the U.S., one can only conclude that they were drawn up by someone with the same mentality as the people who ran the U.S. Bureau of Indian Affairs in the nineteenth century. The Palestinian Arabs were to inhabit areas or zones that bear striking resemblances to the cruel and shameful reservations that relegated the Native Americans to lives of hardship under outside domination. All major security points and water resources were to be under Israeli control. There was no coherent plan for a Palestinian state, since many of the Palestinian areas were separated from each other, surrounded by Israeli encampments and settlements, and crisscrossed by Israeli military highways. Also, these Camp David Accords postponed any meaningful decisions concerning the status of Jerusalem, the Arab "right of return" to areas in present-day Israel that they inhabited before the 1947–1948 Arab-Israeli war, and the fate of the Israeli settlements in the West Bank. These scandalous Israeli proposals, even though they were somewhat modified by pressures from a U.S. government that itself was embarrassed by their gross unfairness, revealed the impossible security situation of Israel if a truly independent Palestinian state came into being. The Camp David negotiations fell victim to President Clinton's lame duck status and the upcoming difficult Israeli parliamentary elections. Prime Minister Barak lost the election to Ariel Sharon, who campaigned on the platform that Barak was soft on the Palestinians and was giving away too much at Camp David. Those who claim that Yasser Arafat failed his people by not grasping this "wonderful" Camp David deal obviously believe that Israel has some kind of historic and moral right to subjugate and control the lives of the Palestinian Arabs. It is very curious that these are the same people who often claim, regardless of any counterargument, that Israel has possession of the moral high ground. In this strange way of thinking, morality is in no way related to one's actual thoughts and actions. If Arafat had signed on at Camp David 2000, he most likely would have been killed by his own people. That outcome might have suited some of his very "moral" enemies among the Israelis and the Americans, but it would have done nothing to lead the region toward peace. In reality, Arafat and the Israeli leadership were not the main problems at the Camp David Summit of 2000. They were the products of the insanity of trying to fit two very different peoples into one very small "country" called Palestine.

The Camp David 2000 Summit did recognize, by its harsh proposals to place many strictures on the Palestinian Arabs, that any independent Arab state in the West Bank, if it were allowed to arm itself with modern weapons, would threaten Israel's security simply by its proximity to Israeli population centers. Hardliners and militants among both the Israelis and the Palestinian Arabs and their allies would have little difficulty or reservations about disrupting any peace arrangement that granted real independence to, or bound into subservience, the West Bank and the Gaza Strip. Let it be clear: *Either the Arabs or the Israelis will have to leave Palestine.* There is no other practical long-term solution. In short, either the highly questionable and morally unjustifiable process of turning Palestine into Israel that was incubated by the British and sustained by the Americans must be brought to completion, or this process must be rescinded and the Jews must end the state of Israel as an independent political entity. If the second option comes to pass, it would seem that very few Israelis would wish to live in a sea of Arabs and Moslems.

Where could the Jews go and find contentment in an independent political state? The countries in Africa and South America would be most unlikely to surrender territory for a new Israeli state. While it is possible that some countries might wish to consider selling territory for a new Israeli state, the payment would have to be huge and probably tied to other programs of aid and technology transfers to the seller nation. This possibility remains to be explored. Most of the countries of Europe are facing serious declines in their birthrates, but latent and overt anti-Jewish and now anti-Semitic feelings against both Arabs and Jews make it highly improbable that these societies would be willing to make any territorial concessions toward a new Israeli state. Most of the Jews probably would not even be welcomed back as new citizens in the European countries that they had left on their way to Israel many years ago. This shameful situation is a reminder that the tragic modern Arab-Israeli conflict is to a large degree the result of the inability of the European Christian countries to resolve in a "Christian way" the presence of a significant number of Jews in their societies.

The United States, Canada, Australia, the Russian Federation, and Kazakhstan are the only other possible places for a new Israeli state. However, none of these five countries has any precedent for surrendering territories to non-indigenous peoples to establish an independent state. The most likely scenario would be that they could offer the Israelis places to settle and opportunities to become citizens of these host countries. Certainly, the demonstrated abilities and hard work of the Israeli people would be inducements for any of these five countries to welcome the Jews. While it is true that the late Soviet dictator Joseph Stalin tinkered with the idea of a kind of "Soviet Palestine" called Birobidzhan in Siberia, north of Manchuria, it is improbable that the leadership of the Russian Federation would be any more willing than Stalin to allow an independent Israeli state to emerge anywhere in its enormous territory. Some might say that an Israeli state north of China might be useful in bringing non-Chinese people into a sparsely settled southern Siberia. However, it seems difficult to imagine that Israelis would want to flock to the remote and landlocked reaches of Siberia or Kazakhstan should land be made available for an independent or autonomous Israeli state. The same problems, in different degrees, would apply to the U.S., Canada, and Australia. No country would be enthusiastic to make land available for an independent Israeli state.

If the Israelis, in the face of unending violence, chronic insecurity, and the real threat posed by the much higher Arab birthrate, are induced to leave Israel and relocate, in some fashion, to other countries or to an independent state elsewhere, how will they be compensated? Monetary compensation would have to run in the area of 550 billion dollars, plus the value of personally held real estate and non-publicly traded businesses. These funds would have to be controlled and distributed by a United Nations commission composed of individuals from non-Arab, non-Moslem, and non-donor countries such as China, Australia, Brazil, New Zealand, and Argentina. The main contributors to this compensation fund would be the chief perpetrators of this unfortunate Israeli nation-building adventure: Great Britain, the U.S., and Jewish groups around the world. Certainly, Israeli military expertise and personnel would be avidly sought after, and would add to the effectiveness of any host country's armed forces. Israeli scientific and entrepreneurial talents would be widely sought after. This solution means that there would be no independent state of Israel. Jerusalem would become an international city under United Nations control, policed by "neutral troops" from such relatively uninvolved countries as China, Brazil, Finland, Mexico, Norway, Sweden, and Venezuela.

The only other solution is the removal of all Palestinian Arabs from the Gaza Strip and areas west of the Jordan River, and their relocation to the present-day Kingdom of Jordan (where Palestinian Arabs already comprise a majority of the population) or other countries willing to receive them. Israeli hardliners have been calling for this for many years, but without substantial compensation. This plan would also conveniently solve the intractable problems of the fate of the Jewish settlements on the West Bank and the Palestinian Arab demand for the "right of return." This demand for the "right of return" on the part of the Arab former residents of present-day Israeli territories mirrors the Israeli policy of the "right of return" to Israel for all Jews throughout the world. As in the first option, Jerusalem would become an international city, with specifics to be discussed below.

What would Israel and its Western backers have to do to bring this option to fruition? If there is to be a permanent settlement of the Arab-Israeli conflict, all parties must be honest and, to a degree, contrite. It is the only way that a new and true atmosphere of confidence and trust can be established. Israel will have to make some very profound and far-reaching admissions concerning the deceptions used on the Arabs and the manipulations used on the British and the Americans in the first half of the twentieth century that led up to the founding of the Israeli state. Israel must discuss the early Zionist attempts to camouflage the deceptive and dishonest policies in regard to the need for the removal of Arab inhabitants from the territories of the future state of Israel. Israel will also have to confess that murderous thuggery and many Zionist terrorist acts were crucial to the establishment of the state of Israel. For example, Etzel murdered at least 130 people who strongly backed the implementation of the St. James Conference White Paper of 1939, which, among other things, clearly revealed the unfair British pro-Zionist policies in Palestine, and called for sharp limits on Jewish immigration and the end of gross favoritism toward the Zionists.[10] David Ben Gurion, the future Israeli prime minister, was deeply troubled by the implications of the St. James Conference White Paper for the future creation of an independent state of Israel. Israel, the "noble victim" and staunch opponent of terrorism, is living proof that terrorism is a practical avenue to attaining political goals. It is the example of Zionist terrorism to which the Islamic terrorists can point as a model of success. Israel exists, in part, because certain elements in the pre-1948 Zionist communities resorted to terrorist acts against the Arabs, and, toward the end of the Mandate, against the British themselves.

The central moral dilemma of the Zionist enterprise in Palestine was that, on the one hand, the Jews espoused liberal European and American values of justice and fair play, which included human rights and national self-determination, yet to be successful in their nation creating, it was necessary to deport and put to flight the Palestinian Arabs and seize their lands and deny them self-determination. These immoral policies and methods used to set up the Jewish state deeply troubled David Ben Gurion and other Zionist leaders of liberal European heritage. Deportations and forced transfers of Arabs were similar to the terrible things that America had done to the native Indians of North America, and that some of the European countries had done to the Jews themselves. It was here that the Jews lost the "moral high ground" that so many Israelis still think they possess. Their methods of bringing Israel into being created a deformed Israel and a tragic Middle East situation.

The British will have to go on the record in regard to their shameful collusion with Zionist extremists in making it possible for the state of Israel to emerge. Britain was not evenhanded; it was grossly pro-Jewish. London must apologize to the Palestinian Arabs for General Montgomery's brutal suppression of the justifiable Arab revolt against Britain's consistently anti-Arab policies. General Montgomery's disgraceful and savage attacks against the Arabs had no counterpart in Britain's attempt to control the post-World War II Zionist terrorist bombings and attacks against the British themselves. The Christian Zionist fantasies of British Prime Ministers David Lloyd George and Ramsay MacDonald, Foreign Secretary Arthur Balfour, and Malcolm MacDonald, as well as the Zionist financial assistance to Winston Churchill and the intrusion of Justice Louis Brandeis into the formulation of American foreign policy, must all be laid bare as vital elements in the creation of the contemporary Middle East disaster. The different British responses to opposition in Palestine from the Arabs and from the Jews enabled the relatively small Zionist forces to be in a far superior position in terms of organization and military experience than the broken Palestinian forces, as well as the Arab ceremonial colonial troops that ineptly tried to suppress the Zionist establishment of the state of Israel.

If the United States wishes to change its badly tarnished image in the eyes of the more than one billion Moslems throughout the world, Washington will have to admit publicly that over the years since World War II, it has, except during the Carter Administration, unfairly favored and backed Israel with massive military, intelligence, financial, and political aid, all out of proportion to the size of Israel's territory and population. The U.S. should also apologize to the Middle Eastern peoples for not encouraging democratic movements and ideas in the region and for not seriously urging gradual reforms among the monarchies of the Middle East. The United States should also admit that its administrations, through the years, have been under intense pressure to favor Israel because of heavy Jewish campaign contributions and the importance of the "Jewish vote" in certain crucial states. If the U.S. wants peace in the Middle East, then Washington must participate in the admission of reprehensible deeds by all of the involved parties, and cease trying to solve the problems of the Middle East through military attacks that breed suicidal martyrs.

Great Britain and the United States will have to come off their high horses and apologize to the Palestinian Arabs for treating them with dishonor and with disrespect. Until this is done, attempts by Washington or London to hold themselves out as honest brokers in any serious Middle East settlement have to be viewed as incredible acts of self-delusion and dishonesty. The smug belief that the U.S. and Britain could endlessly hoodwink the "ignorant" Arabs and other Moslems by mouthing concepts of evenhandedness while in reality carrying on a long-running love affair with Israel should have been shattered forever by the kerosene-laden flying Molotov cocktails of the September 11 attacks. The Arabs and the Islamic militants were not fooled by the misleading statements of fairness concerning the Middle East that were made over the years by the United States and Britain. Only a Western leader like President Carter, by the sheer power of his personal integrity and honesty, could briefly bridge the huge trust gap between the Islamic countries and the West.

The Palestinians and the Moslem groups that support them and those who use the plight of the Palestinians for their own propaganda purposes will have to apologize for and put an end to the widespread teaching of hatred toward their Semitic brothers and sisters (the Jews), who, because of their attempts to escape the many horrific atrocities inflicted upon them over the centuries by European peoples, came to see Palestine as a hope and as a possible refuge. Moslems must openly condemn the use of Islamic texts for the purpose of causing harm and death to Jews and other peoples, both Islamic and non-Islamic. All the major religious groups—the Jews, the Christians, and the Moslems—must proclaim that the use of their religious teachings and traditions to justify acts of violence discredits those religions. The cunning use of the Hebrew Bible and other writings to justify the seizure of another people's homeland through deception and lies is dishonest and shameful. Is it condoned in the Hebrew tradition to think of another people as inferior and to treat them in a degrading manner? In Islam, does God condone the hatred of another people (the Jews—the Semitic brothers and sisters of the Arabs) and call for their expulsion and murder? The sad inability of the various Christian denominations to adhere to the teachings of Jesus Christ in regard to the treatment of the peoples of different religious, racial, and ethnic backgrounds is reason for reflection and prayer. Furthermore, it must always be remembered that there is no conclusive historical or scientific evidence that any of these religious texts came from anywhere but religious leaders who may have had self-serving interests in mind in addition to deeply held religious beliefs.

Islamic demands that all lands once occupied by Moslem forces and then lost must be recaptured are as unacceptable as Zionist claims that all lands promised to them in the Hebrew Bible must be a part of a reconstituted Israel. Should the once-Christian lands of Asia Minor (modern-day Turkey) and most of the Middle East (including Egypt, Syria, and most of North Africa) be brought back under Christian control and occupation? Should the Balkans, Spain, and Sicily, all of which were once conquered by the Moslems, be viewed as legitimate targets for Islamic re-conquest? There are religious zealots, political opportunists, and glory-hungry militarists on all sides of this conflict who seek to use religion as a cover for their more base cravings.

If the second option out of this tragedy is pursued, the UK, the U.S., and Israel will have to pay approximately 550 billion dollars to the Palestinians, the Kingdom of Jordan, and other host countries in the Middle East. This is the price to end the killings and the cruel disruptions of so many lives caused by the establishment of Israel. The Palestinian Arabs will be justly compensated for giving up their ancestral lands in exchange for new homes and a new life free from Israeli control. Ultimately, it is the only way to stop the killings and to reduce the high military expenditures on all sides. It is the most peaceful and least expensive way out of an insolvable tangle of hatred and revenge. The historic mistake that London made, once again aptly described by Arthur Koestler as "one nation [Britain] promising to another nation [the Jews] the land of a third nation [the Palestinians]," must stand for all time as a supreme folly that all statesmen must never forget. Starting with this settlement, Israel will pay for Palestinian lands rather than, under the shameful cloak of specious scriptural authority, steal Arab lands or occupy them with illegal settlements. After all, the followers of Moses should be aware that it is against the Ten Commandments to steal. Also, Israel, while gaining much land and improving its security, will probably have to pay much more than the UK and the U.S. on a per-capita basis because of its expanded territory. There will be other costs for Israel. Jerusalem must be made into an international city, with a land corridor to the Jordanian border. The city and the land corridor must be under United Nations civil and military control. Access to all religious, cultural, and historic sites must be guaranteed by the United Nations. The cost of this operation would be borne by Israel, Britain, the U.S., and Jordan. Israel would have to undergo UN nuclear inspections and sign the 1970 Nuclear Nonproliferation Treaty. The American hypocrisy in demanding inspections of Iranian nuclear facilities while Israel has been allowed to develop nuclear weapons with French assistance stands as another example of the U.S. favoring Israel over the Arabs by means of its UN Security Council veto. If no other Middle East state possessed nuclear weapons, then Israel would have to dispose of these weapons. The Middle East (from North Africa through Turkey to the western border of Pakistan) should become a nuclear-weapons free zone.

At first, there will be a great deal of denial and resistance on all sides to these proposals. It will not take a long time for the Palestinian Arabs to see this plan as the best way to resolve an insolvable situation that in the past has resulted in and in the future can only invite continued chaos and terrible violence for both the Arabs and the Israelis. If the Palestinian Arabs wish to have a new, better, and far less violent existence for their families, then this option offers a very attractive opportunity for them. The new towns and far superior amenities that will be built in Jordan and elsewhere will make the plan more easily acceptable to the vast majority of the current Palestinian Arab inhabitants of Gaza, the West Bank, and even Israel itself. The large-scale construction activities and infrastructure improvements that would ensue in the wake of this plan will create an uplifting of the Jordanian economy and bring prosperity to many citizens. This assumes that the Israelis are willing to gamble that they will not be swamped demographically by their own Arab population in present-day Israel. If neither the buyout of the Israelis nor the buyout of the Palestinian Arabs is realized, then the existing situation of endless hostility, attacks, and killings will go on indefinitely. Eventually, Israel, through its program of settlements in the West Bank, will impose a de facto "one-state solution" with the certainty that the Palestinian Arabs soon will outnumber the Jews in an expanded Israeli state. The only ways to counter this looming reality will be either to commence a program of ruthless ethnic cleansing or to impose non-democratic rule over its Arab citizens. In other words, the two original options are giving both the Israelis and the Arabs politically incorrect exit strategies that very few have been willing to discuss openly. One of these two options—the buy-out of the Israelis or the buyout of the Palestinian Arabs—offers the only hope for a measured cessation of the violence leading to a permanent peace. Some diehard militants on both sides will have to be incarcerated or killed to end this tragically mistaken venture in nation creating.

In some quarters, this second plan (the buyout of the Palestinian Arabs) will be viewed as rewarding a nation that employed deception and the tactic that "might makes right." Certainly, the early and later Islamic conquests could be viewed in that light. The European conquests of North and South America and Russia's conquest of northern Asia (Siberia) are other examples of "might making right." However, this plan exacts a very stiff price from all those who participated in and benefited from this particular instance of "might making right." The reality of an escape from poverty and violence and the promise of a much higher living standard could prove to be very strong inducements to resettle outside of a dead-end existence in Gaza and the West Bank.

This second plan can work because, ultimately, all the involved parties will come out ahead. The Palestinian Arabs will gain peace and prosperity in nearby new homes with very significant material advances. They can begin to live normal lives with good future prospects. Jordan will have to be rewarded for its participation in this option. The Israelis will gain a far superior defensive situation and the hope of eventually developing normal economic relationships with their Arab neighbors. Israel's defense budget could be greatly reduced and its economy could recover to a state of normalcy. The internationalization of Jerusalem and the creation of the UN-controlled corridor from Jordan to Jerusalem would mean that everyone would have free access to the city without the discomfort or humiliation of going through the customs of a hostile country. The Jews would be able to celebrate their holidays in Jerusalem, as would the Moslems and the Christians. An internationalized Jerusalem would not include most of the post-1967 suburbs. Jordan would gain many new citizens, who would not be arriving as impoverished refugees. Jordan, Egypt, Syria, and other recipient nations of the Middle East would be able to reduce the burden of defense spending to the benefit of their economies. Tensions throughout the region would be reduced and the U.S. and the UK could extricate themselves from what has been till now an insolvable dilemma, while at the same time developing more normal relations with most of the countries of the Middle East and the extended Islamic world. The only real losers in all of this will be the international munitions dealers and the arms manufacturing countries.

Now that there are these two options before the participants in the Arab-Israeli conflict, it is necessary to confront the major remaining ethnic problem in the Middle East: the statelessness of the Kurds. There will be no overall peace in the Middle East until the unfinished business of the inept Western dismemberment of the Ottoman Empire's Middle East possessions is finally resolved. The Kurds inhabit the northeastern corner of Syria, the southeastern expanses of Turkey, the northwestern fringe of Iran, and about half of the old Ottoman province of Mosul (the present-day northern bulge of Iraq). In all these regions, the Kurds predominate and all together comprise a population of more than twenty-five million people, with approximately fourteen to fifteen million living in southeastern Turkey. The recent historical context of this situation has been the brutal and bloody Turkish suppression of the culture, language, and political aspirations of the Kurds of Turkey. The role of the U.S. in militarily, politically, and diplomatically supporting these genocidal policies of successive Turkish regimes is one of America's most shameful, disgraceful, and hypocritical involvements. For decades, Britain and the U.S. have hidden behind the "fig leaf" of tolerating horrific Turkish abuses of human rights and decency in order to maintain Turkish support against the USSR. This lame excuse for backing brutal and at times genocidal Turkish regimes never made sense, considering that Russia has been Turkey's greatest and deadliest military and political enemy for centuries. In reality, Turkey had no choice but to ally itself with the U.S. during the Cold War. There was no reason for the United States to tolerate Turkish atrocities. If anything, America had very strong leverage available to pressure for meaningful reforms that would have benefited all the citizens of Turkey. Now that the USSR has disappeared and United States relations with Russia are more normalized, America still does not have the moral fortitude and courage to demand that Turkey adhere to the standards of the civilized world or suffer reductions in aid and exclusion from Western organizations.

The fair, humane, democratic, and long overdue solution to the Kurdish situation is the creation of a Kurdish state encompassing all of the abovementioned Kurdish-inhabited areas. If Turkey cannot bring itself to follow the example of the Czechs in acknowledging the peaceful wishes of the Slovak people to have their own state, then it is difficult to see a place for Turkey in the EU or in NATO. As in the case of the brutal suppression of the Albanians by the Serbs in Kosovo, the more than thirty-year savage Turkish war to prevent the Kurds from escaping Turkish subjugation must result in Ankara losing all claims to the Kurdish regions of eastern Turkey. After all, the U.S. is supposed to be the champion of self-determination for major ethnic and national groups—or does this not apply to "allies" of the U.S., who are allowed to make a mockery of everything America claims to represent? The Kurdish areas of Iraq should be the beginnings of this new Kurdish state. If the Turkish Army invades Iraq to stop this development, then Ankara must be held accountable by the European Union, the United Nations, and NATO, the military alliance of free and democratic states. It would be very helpful if the U.S. spoke up forcefully and refrained from surrendering to the base instincts of right-wing Turkish nationalists and their attack-dog generals who head the huge military machine that America so foolishly helped to create. Turkey, like other outlaw states, should be put under sanctions until those responsible for atrocities are sent to the World Criminal Court at The Hague. Most Turks, being more sensible than the traditional ruling circles of the country, will see real advantages in joining the democratic societies of the European Union rather than trying to maintain a reactionary, colonial-type subjugation of a neighboring Sunni Moslem people who are part of one of the larger nations in the Middle East. There is always resistance to confronting political realities, but that is what a democracy is all about. Like Russia after the end of the USSR, Turkey would be free from the heavy financial and political burdens of garrisoning hostile and mutinous areas. This will enable Turkey to reduce its very heavy military expenditures and redeploy its many resources to elevating the low living standards of the long-suffering Turkish people.

The Turkish people's recent overwhelming reelection of a government that is not a part of the traditional ruling cliques, is not under the thumb of the Turkish generals, and has displayed an independence from self-centered American aims in the Middle East, reveals a desire on the part of the Turkish people to create a real democracy. The

United States is not viewed as a true friend of Turkey, but as a manipulator and user of Turkey for the perceived interests of the U.S. Though it may seem most unlikely, both Iran and Syria, in time, will see the righteousness and advantages of ending the needless subjugation of a potentially friendly neighboring Moslem people (the Kurds). Another possibility is that Syria and Iran may find it expedient to fund the transfer of any willing Kurds from their countries to the new Kurdish state. While this line of thinking may seem farfetched to many, the opportunity for the "dawning of enlightenment" in this matter will probably come during regime changes in both Syria and Iran. It is possible that Syria might find it expedient to surrender its small Kurdish areas as part of a general Middle East settlement in which Damascus would regain a demilitarized Golan Heights.

The entire Middle East will be much better off with highly homogeneous major political entities. The remainder of Iraq will survive as a smaller Arab state, still possessing vast oil riches and, hopefully, a laboratory for Moslem sectarian coexistence. Patience and leadership on the part of the European Union, the United Nations, the United States, and the Russian Federation will be required to see these vital changes to completion over a period of many years. Western and Middle East countries working closely in the United Nations must end the denial of human rights and respond to the yearnings for self-determination on the part of minorities in the Middle East. It is the best hope and the fundamental means for achieving peace and prosperity in the region. In contrast, all previous attempts to resolve the Middle East quagmire, as well as the plans of the Bush II Administration for the "democratization" of the Middle East, make little sense in that they are based on maintaining the political mistakes that were made by the former colonial powers that carved out the administrative entities that became some of the present-day countries of the region. These administrative entities, in some very important instances, did not take into consideration the wishes and realities of certain religious and ethnic groups. Democracy cannot be imposed from above by outside powers unless those powers plan to occupy the country with huge numbers of troops (exceeding 1.5 million men) for ten or more years. Short of a world war, such thinking is entirely impractical and vastly expensive. The continued failure of American and British policies in the Middle East is assured by Washington's and London's stubborn adherence to policies that perpetuate Israeli domination of the Palestinian Arabs, Turkish suppression of the Kurds in southeastern Turkey, and Turkish veto power, backed by the U.S., over the aspirations of the Kurds in Iraq and elsewhere.

The creation of a no-fly zone over the Kurdish areas of northern Iraq after the first Gulf War, and the relative calm that came in its wake, were part of an attempt to restrict the actions of the Iraqi air force and, on the part of America, to atone for the callous abandonment of the Kurds to the savage reprisals of the Saddam regime. At the time, the U.S. had irresponsibly encouraged the Iraqi Kurds to "rise up" and overthrow Saddam's rule over the Kurds. However, the U.S. and its allies failed to send any meaningful military assistance to the Kurdish anti-Saddam insurgents. The United States, Great Britain, Turkey, and Israel have displayed, in varying shades, the same colonial arrogance of power in the Middle East that the eighteenth- and nineteenth-century imperial powers displayed in arbitrarily dividing ethnic and religious groups in the Americas, Africa, and Asia. The concept of "divide, conquer, and rule" did not go out of fashion. These irrational and tragic political creations may have satisfied the wishes of the European power brokers, but they eventually resulted in chronic political instability, brutally repressive regimes, endless regional wars, frightening massacres, and periodic genocides. While the Western powers are not fully responsible for some of these terrible events, there is no question that their inadequate and irresponsible policies of failing, in most cases, to prepare competent native administrations, disciplined armed forces, and a sufficient number of educated citizens to carry on responsibly contributed in major ways to these very unfortunate events. To be responsible and successful imperialists and colonial masters, it is necessary not only to conquer, rule, and exploit, but also, educate, elevate, and lead the ruled toward a superior way of life.

CHAPTER VIII
WHY AMERICA CANNOT CHANGE ITS FAILED POLICIES

In order for America to review thoroughly and to reorder objectively its disastrous policies in the Middle East, it will be necessary to have a political earthquake in the United States. Neither the Republicans nor the Democrats have shown any meaningful desire to lead the U.S. away from an election system that is largely controlled by an ocean of lobby-directed campaign contributions. The two major parties have been central to the catastrophe of the buying of America's government on both the national and state levels. The financial power of the lobby groups must be eliminated from the electoral process in America. This can only be accomplished through publicly funded election campaigns. Our current political leaders, because nearly all of them are creatures of the existing system, are either unwilling or unable to end this national disgrace of the "greatest democracy on earth" being, in reality, little more than a greedy and unsavory plutocracy (rule by the rich), hiding behind a "democratic" fig leaf. After all, if the election system were freed from the domination of plutocratic lobbyists, our current politicians would be placed on a much more even playing field against challengers, who would not be forced to drop out of the race because they failed to please the plutocratic money brokers.

Under a publicly funded system, candidates must not be allowed to use their own personal or family money or money from any other source, including the Internet. No funds from lobbies, corporations, labor unions, social groups, private individuals, private or public foundations, political action groups, interest groups, nonprofit groups, religious groups, or charitable groups can be used in political campaigns. Furthermore, these organizations and individuals cannot use paid individuals to secure the valid signatures required to qualify for the primaries. Violations of these rules must be met with heavy fines and jail terms. Lobby groups would be able to present their cases to the elected officials and candidates without the potential threats of denying financial support to elected officials and candidates. Groups focusing on various campaign issues would be free to voice their views in the media but must not refer to or mention any candidates or political parties or groups. The sponsors of the ads would have to be identified. These ads would be privately funded and could cover virtually any subject matter. Regular media news outlets, news programs, and talk shows would not be governed by these rules.

At both the senatorial and gubernatorial levels, the candidates would have to qualify for public funding by having volunteers secure at least 75,000 valid signatures from registered voters. Candidates for the House of Representatives would need to secure at least 25,000 valid signatures. Candidates who secured the minimum number of signatures would receive the same amount of public money for their primary campaigns to use in any way they thought to be advantageous to their cause. The qualifying senatorial and gubernatorial candidates would each receive two million dollars, and the qualifying candidates for the House of Representatives would receive four hundred thousand dollars. Some adjustments in the number of signatures and in the amounts of campaign funds may be made for very small or large states.

Campaign forums and debates would be orchestrated by the election commission. A candidate receiving less than 20 percent of the vote in the primary would be disqualified from the final election. Political parties would be allowed to participate only after the primary elections. Political parties would be under the same funding restrictions as the candidates. In order for a political party to qualify for public funding, it would have to have as its candidate someone who qualified in the primary. The public funding for the political parties during non-presidential–year elections would be fifty million dollars per election year. Each candidate for the Senate or for governor would be funded the amount of five million dollars for an election. Each candidate for the House of Representatives would be funded seven hundred thousand dollars for an election. These amounts would be adjusted with the consumer price index. Any left-over funds would have to be returned to the independent federal agency that funds elections (possibly the Internal Revenue Service). The period for collecting valid signatures to qualify for the primary would be three months. The primary election period would be three months. Final election campaign periods would be restricted to three months for the House of Representatives and three months for senatorial and gubernatorial aspirants.

In the presidential elections, the country would be divided into five groups of ten states each. Each group of ten states should be composed of a regional cluster rather than a scattered group across the country. In any event, the candidate for president would have campaign workers secure signatures in the group of states that included the candidate's home state. Limited funds would be granted for each candidate to secure the minimum number of signatures to qualify for the regional primaries. A sum of one hundred thousand dollars for each candidate should suffice for the regional signature campaigns. This money should be doled out in stages as the candidates show that they indeed are seriously obtaining valid signatures of voters. In order to qualify for the regional primaries, a candidate would have to secure the signatures of at least three hundred fifty thousand registered voters. The campaign period would be three months. The two highest vote-getters in each regional primary would go on to the semi-national primaries.

In the semi-national primaries, the nation would be divided into two groups of twenty-five states each. Each group would be made up of a division of the United States into an eastern group and a western group of approximately similar numbers of citizens. The government would fund each qualifying candidate in the semi-national primaries to the tune of five million dollars. The two highest vote-getting candidates in each semi-national primary would go on to the national primary. The government would fund each candidate in the national primary to the tune of thirty-five million dollars. The two highest vote-getting candidates in the national primary would then go on to the general election. The government would make available one hundred million dollars to each presidential candidate for campaign expenses. At this point, the political parties would become active, and as long as they were affiliated with one of the two surviving candidates, would receive seventy-five million dollars for campaign purposes. The rare unaffiliated candidate would split the $75,000,000.00 with the political party that had no presidential candidate. Any political party that is affiliated with at least 15% of the surviving general election candidates running for governor, the House of Representatives and the Senate would be eligible for the sum of $37,000,000.00 even if the party was not affiliated with a presidential candidate. The government would organize a number of campaign forums and debates. The period allotted for the securing of regional presidential nominating signatures would be three months. The election period for the regional primaries would be limited to three months. The election period for the semi-national primaries would be limited to three months. The period for the national primary would be limited to three months. The presidential election period would be limited to three months. This system will eliminate the distracting fundraising efforts and obscene spending on campaigns that have made American presidential elections and party nominating conventions appear more like carnivals than serious business. Some industries, such as the media and the convention and hotel businesses, will find that the elections will not be as big a bonanza as before. Party conventions will become more oriented toward platform and issue development than political hoopla.

Because most of the current incumbent elected officials achieved their positions through the existing corrupt election system, it is unlikely that they would wish to eliminate the system that they have mastered and that enabled them to win their positions of power. This understandable human wish to cling to power most likely necessitates that electoral reform be done by referendum on the state level and eventually culminate in an amendment to the U.S. Constitution. This will be a slow process, and in the interim, the United States will stumble from one crisis to another, since its foreign policies reflect the narrow and selfish interests of plutocratic lobbyists and quite infrequently the real interests of the American people. In truth, not only are people around the world victims of the greed and power-seeking of some plutocratic groups in America, but so are the hapless American citizens, whose young people are often sent to fight and die in wars that serve the wishes of ideological minorities as well as the plutocrats.

The lobbyists themselves, except in a relatively small number of cases, have not done anything illegal. Actually, they have become masters at playing the Washington money game of keeping the politicians thinking their way lest large amounts of campaign money end up in the campaign coffers of a challenger in the next election. It is also quite likely that certain politicians foster this corrupt election system to perpetuate their own office-holding by manipulating the lobbyists for all the money that they can get out of them. Lobby groups such as the banking industry, the investment industry, the petroleum industry, the pharmaceutical industry, JINSA (Jewish Institute for National Security Affairs), the farm lobby, the gun lobby, and the dairy lobby, among many others, are complicit in America's current domestic political mess and Washington's ongoing foreign policy quagmires. All of these lobby groups are playing the corrupt American political and economic games by the existing "legal" rules. The United States cannot bring its great strengths to bear on the huge problems that it faces while its attention is being distracted and its resources squandered on the ill-conceived, self-centered, and self-benefiting schemes of some of the lobbies.

What makes the big impact on America's Middle East policies are the power, money, and influence of the petroleum industry and the many pro-Israel lobbies. This not to say that the petroleum lobby always gets its way or that its interests are always contrary to the interests of the United States. Certainly, the petroleum lobby has not necessarily been in favor of open American support for Israel. It and the American people suffered from the U.S. backing of Israel in the 1973 Arab-Israeli War, which, while Israel did prevail, ended up resulting in the expropriation of American oil interests in Saudi Arabia and other Arab oil-producing states, and probably contributed to the overthrow of the Shah of Iran in 1979. The influence of the U.S. on the Middle East oil producers has never recovered, and it is only our generous distribution of aid funds and grants that enables the Arabs to tolerate America on a minimal level. The United States' role has diminished to playing one side against another (e.g., U.S. backing of Saddam Hussein against the Iranians—a monster created, in part, by United States intervention in Iranian domestic politics) or playing on one state's fears of the intentions of its neighbor (Saddam's Iraq versus the Emirates, Saddam's Iraq versus Kuwait, the Arab Emirates versus Iran, and Saudi Arabia versus Iran). One might add that this cycle of potential contemporary regional aggression between Moslem Middle Eastern states was contributed to by America's unfortunate meddling in Iranian domestic affairs (the aggressive desire to maintain control of the Iranian oil industry by overthrowing the Mossadegh government in 1953, resulting in the emergence in 1979 of the virulently anti-American and anti-Western government of contemporary Iran). Once again, the U.S. government's attempt to serve the interests of certain lobbies (the oil lobby and JINSA) cost the United States dearly and embroiled us deeper in the endless tangle of Middle East problems for which the U.S. has no solutions.

The well-known pro-Israel lobbies, which include the American Enterprise Institute, the Centre for Strategic and International Studies, the American Israel Public Affairs Committee, the Zionist Organization of America, the Bradley Foundation, the Olin Foundation, and others, are linked into a pro-Israel umbrella lobby called the Jewish Institute for National Security Affairs (JINSA). It is not difficult to understand that a network of worldwide pro-Israel organizations is working in much the same manner, only with much more money and contacts, as an earlier "nonexistent" Jewish network of money moguls who apparently wielded much pro-Israel influence over British and American political leaders during the first half of the twentieth century. The phenomenal growth of the power of the pro-Israel lobbies and the longtime strong influence of the petroleum industry lobby over the U.S. executive and legislative branches of government make it impossible for America to take decisive action to solve the Arab-Israeli conflict or to act as a truly neutral, honest broker capable of evenhandedness in resolving the serious problems of the region. For the pro-Israel "politically correct police," even the term "evenhandedness" must be smeared with the emotionally charged accusation of "anti-Semitism." In this intellectually bankrupt and dishonest approach, virtually anyone who supports any Palestinian Arab position is nearly always suspected of anti-Semitism, in spite of the fact that the Arabs are by far the largest Semitic group in the world.

Another issue that must be confronted by the American people and their elected representatives is that in the U.S. Departments of Defense and State, there are some influential senior and junior officials who have been lobbyists for Israel or for American and foreign-based pro-

Israel groups. These individuals may sincerely believe that they do not have a conflict of interests and that the interests of Israel and the U.S in the Middle East are virtually identical. People with such backgrounds, whether they be with Israel, the Arab states, or any foreign country, should not be in sensitive and influential positions where they can directly affect the making of policy decisions in an area where they have committed themselves to the interests of a foreign state (e.g., Israel). Recent statements by such individuals to the effect that the 2003 invasion of Iraq would lead the way to the emergence of truly democratic regimes throughout the Middle East seem overly optimistic. They reveal either their naive and shallow understanding of these societies and their respective heritages or their uncompromising desire to use U.S. foreign policies to insure what they feel are the interests of Israel. Ignorance of the history of the Middle East and uncompromising favoritism to any one state in the region must never form the basis for American policies. Democracy is an issue for the Islamic peoples of the Middle East, but it is not yet the burning issue for the vast majority. The crucial issues for the Arab citizens are justice and fairness—not that they encounter much justice and fairness in their everyday lives. However, they are very resentful when they feel that they or their Moslem neighbors in the region have been treated by outsiders (Westerners, Israelis, and Turks) in a manner that denies justice and fairness.

The important matter for them is one that Washington keeps claiming is not the burning issue in the Middle East. America must listen to the Islamic peoples of the Middle East and realize that the burning issue is that they wish to control the magnitude of the intrusion of the West into their societies. In their view, a big part of that intrusion has been the conspiracy of the West in the creation of Israel. They do not see Israel as a Middle Eastern nation, but as latter-day "crusader state" representing the ultimate interests of the United States, Britain, the European Union, and what the Arabs view as a worldwide Jewish conspiracy. Terrorism will not end until there is a decision between options one and two of this presentation. All other attempts to resolve the Arab-Israeli conflict have been doomed to consistent failure.

The inability of the U.S. and Britain to confront and deal rationally with these painful realities has unfortunately characterized the reactions of both countries to the terrorist threat. The September 11 attacks so traumatized a naive and self-assured America that its government has been left grasping at moralistic explanations for those events. From near oblivion, discussions of "evil" have made an impressive comeback. A harsh and unspeakable reality is that the World Trade Center attacks were aimed not only at America's preeminent business and communications center (New York City), but also at the city that has come to symbolize the power and success of the American and even the world Jewish communities. It should come as no surprise that the World Trade Center complex, prior to the September 11 attacks, had been the focus of a well-publicized long and bitter battle for control of the complex between two very prominent Jewish-American real estate moguls. Many militant and not-so-militant Moslems in many countries considered the World Trade Center complex to be the most overt symbol of what they claim is a "Judeo-American conspiracy" to dominate the world. Many Arabs, Moslems, and non-Moslems in America and throughout the world are convinced that the United States and Great Britain, in the final analysis, are controlled by networks of Jews who dominate the economies, the media companies, the professions, and ultimately the governments of both countries. The U.S. and UK, in brushing aside these allegations as absurd, have done nothing either to disprove these widely accepted charges or to come to grips with them in meaningful discussions and investigations.

Probably the most glaring example of the American media's inability to handle realistically the reporting of the meaning of terrorism was *Time* magazine's cowardly and dishonest naming of Mayor Rudolf Giuliani as its 2001 "Person of the Year." This statement is in no way to detract from the courageous job that Mayor Giuliani did under extremely difficult circumstances. Even though *Time* magazine could not admit it, the person who most changed the world "for good or evil" was Osama bin Laden through the worldwide terrorist movements that his al Qaeda organization has inspired. Osama bin Laden could not receive the "Person of the Year" award because it was believed that he orchestrated the profound humiliation of the only country that still thought of itself as a "superpower" or "hyperpower." He did this utilizing relatively low technology (flying Molotov cocktails) in the bombing of the American military headquarters (the Pentagon), by bombing the Twin Towers in New York City, and by causing major changes in the free lifestyle and security consciousness of peoples in many countries around the world. America was so deeply harmed psychologically by bin Laden and his associates that the U.S. responded with ill-conceived preemptive attacks against two Moslem nations (Afghanistan and Iraq) with inconclusive and highly questionable results. Whether he is alive or dead, how much more of a success could bin Laden be? He has profoundly humiliated his "Great Satan" (America), and because of America's furious attempts at revenge by invading Afghanistan and Iraq, there has taken place a vast growth of anti-Americanism throughout the Moslem world as well as in many non-Moslem areas of the globe. Sadly, thanks to the George W. Bush Administration, very few Americans have any idea why they were attacked and what, if anything, can be done to defuse the huge growth in anti-American sentiments that the policies of the Bush and Cheney government have allowed to run wild. The U.S. has had no realistic plan to counter what is a worldwide public relations disaster.

In terms of the Middle East situation and the terrorist threats to the U.S. and its friends and interests around the world, Washington must not continue to deceive itself into believing that the Arab-Israeli conflict is not a major "sparkplug" issue for the Arabs and, increasingly, most Moslems. Attempts to portray the current Moslem-Western standoff as primarily a struggle between civilizations or religions rather than the burning issue of politics that it is for Arab countries is blindness on the part of America and Britain. Conflicts between civilizations or religions are at best secondary or background issues for a world inundated with Western and, in particular, American cultural and media influences. U.S. government claims that the terrorists are trying to destroy the "American way of life" are unconvincing and convoluted at best. Does anyone really believe that Moslem fundamentalists and reactionaries can recruit large numbers of potential terrorists and appeal successfully to an enormous and varied general public in the Islamic world by charging that America's ideas of freedom, human dignity, and self-determination are threats to Moslems everywhere? While there certainly do exist fanatical Moslem groups, the vast majority of people in the Middle East and throughout the world actually desire to partake of these Western ideas of human dignity and freedom. You cannot recruit people to a cause by denouncing the things that people would like to see more of in their own societies. Ideas of freedom, justice, fairness, and human dignity are not the enemies of Islamic peoples. The U.S. policies of favoring Israel and corrupt and repressive Arab regimes that deny freedom and dignity to the Palestinian Arabs and other Moslem and Christian peoples of the Middle East and South Asia are, however, definitely seen as great enemies. For the United States to change its image, it must begin to live up to its ideals.

Britain and the U.S., during the last half century, by their callous and freedom-denying policies in Moslem lands, have created fertile circumstances for the growth of anger and hatred toward America and its allies. These policies, including the tragically mistaken 2003 invasion of Iraq, have greatly assisted the recruitment efforts of militant anti-Western groups throughout the Islamic countries. The most serious enemy of the United States is not the terrorist threat; America's greatest enemy and a dagger pointing at its heart is its own corrupt and bought political system. Because U.S. governments are beholden to the lobbying groups and their campaign contributions, Washington has been unable to formulate policies for the Middle East that would defend and protect America by being based on the ideas annunciated by the founders of the U.S. and elaborated upon in President Woodrow Wilson's somewhat idealistic "Fourteen Points." The United States must try, as much as possible, to live up to its famous principles and stop being hoodwinked by messianic visions of biblical restorations, mass conversions of Jews and Moslems to Christianity during "Second Comings," and divine retributions for all who disagree with "God's position." If America continues to seek answers to and guidance for its Middle East problems in "holy scriptures," Washington will continue to find itself on the same unsound and unfruitful ground as its Koran-quoting militant Moslem adversaries and its Hebrew Bible-quoting militant Jewish allies. The fundamental basis of the Arab-Israeli conflict is political and not religious. Modern Israel was founded mainly by secular socialists. Unfortunately, there are many religious opportunists in Christianity, Islam, and Judaism who have taken advantage of the failings of America foreign policies in the region.

The United States and Britain must listen earnestly to their few remaining Arab and Moslem friends. These include some of the reactionary leaders that we support and who are themselves threatened with replacement by militant Islamic extremists. These friends are not lying when they tell American leaders to wake up to the centrality of the Arab-Israeli conflict. Most of our European allies have been much more willing to confront the harsh reality that Islamic terrorist groups would not be a major problem if the Arab-Israeli conflict did not exist. Instead, America's crude and unsophisticated kneejerk responses, which rely heavily on physically and militarily defeating the opponents of mistaken U.S. Middle East policies, are like trying to kill off a swarm of hornets with rifle shots. Certainly, some of the hornets (terrorists) will be killed by rifle fire, but the rifleman is never going to be able to wipe out the swarm with bullets. Israel has tried harsh military strikes and reprisals for years, only to face more and more terrorists. Since the September 11, 2001 attacks, many Israelis and Americans of Jewish background have said that "now America knows what Israel has been experiencing." From the Arab point of view, it is only right that the U.S. should now know, for America has been taking Israel's side for many years. Unfortunately, the U.S. deserves to experience Israel's tribulations as long as Washington continues to follow Israel's discredited policies and methods. Until very recently, again with the exception of President Carter's efforts, has the U.S. viewed the Palestinians as anything but a pathetic and defeated people who simply cause trouble for our ally Israel? After all, America responds to Israeli transgressions with a mere slap on the wrist. Until lately, it was considered "politically incorrect" to subject Israel to the same objective analysis as was supposed to be employed on all countries, including the U.S. itself.

As far back as President Truman's administration, we have witnessed the curious and suspicious phenomenon of many American presidents, during their inaugural speeches, pledging to defend a foreign state (Israel), even during peaceful times. Similar pronouncements of support for Israel have been made for many years by senators and congressmen. One can safely surmise that these presidents, senators, and congressmen and their political parties were looking for continued financial support from the pro-Israel lobby groups. Is it any wonder that many elements in Palestine and other parts of the Islamic world rejoiced at the September 11 attacks as a long-overdue comeuppance for a country that thought it was cleverly supporting, militarily, diplomatically, and economically, the enemy and tormentor of the Palestinian Arabs? Many Moslems in the world who view

America as arrogant and hypocritical shared these feelings. The ability of the September 11 terrorists to strike across the oceans into the U.S. heartland has raised them to mythic proportions in the eyes of many who have resented the power, wealth, and feelings of cultural superiority of the United States. If at some point America could to a greater degree substitute humility and compassion for arrogance, military attacks, and economic domination, it could disarm many of its most vocal critics.

Only the end of the tyranny of lobby money over U.S. politicians will enable Washington to reinvigorate its foreign policies with the values that once made America seem to be the "best hope of the world." Publicly funded political campaigns are also the only hope for reinvigorating America's domestic politics and ending the national disgrace of the greatest "democracy" on earth having degenerated into an odious plutocracy and into a government of politicians, most of whom must sell themselves to the lobbies to stay in office. Does the U.S., in its Middle East policies, stand for anything but the interests of its dominant lobby groups? If it does, the American government certainly hides it well. The United States talks about freedom, self-determination, human rights, and human dignity, but is allied to Islamic states where all these fine-sounding ideas are violated repeatedly and have been for over half a century. Taking precedence over all other considerations in the Middle East for the United States are the uninterrupted flow of petroleum and the protection of the interests of Israel.

Since America has more influence and power than any other single country in the world, its foreign policies have inordinate impacts throughout the world. If the "world leader" claims to represent a better way through its widely admired values and principles but in the conduct of its foreign policies frequently violates those admired ideas, then Washington will be seen as opportunistic, hypocritical, and unfit to lead the world to a better era. Under these circumstances, America will be viewed correctly as simply following all the previous discredited "world leaders" who offered little that was new beyond the style of their arrogance and their camouflaged desires for riches and control. The U.S. "fig leaf" of attempting to substitute indirect economic domination for overt political control and physical occupation fools very few in the Middle East. When this "fig leaf" policy fails to produce acceptable results, the U.S. may resort to military force. Clearly there are many unsophisticated and surprisingly uninformed policymakers in Washington who believe that the rest of the world has no choice but to fall in behind the U.S., regardless of Washington's policies. It should be remembered that among free people and also among free nations, a leader is followed and honored because the leader is seen as acting wisely and fairly. Stubbornness and narrow-mindedness are usually signs of the inability to process new and unpleasant information and new realities. In free settings, leaders do not coerce or threaten their allies. Truth can only be achieved in circumstances of free discussion and open dissent, with respect for all who act responsibly.

The United States did not act wisely and fairly with many of its European allies in the buildup to the 2003 invasion of Iraq. The raw fury that has characterized the U.S. government's response to the September 11 attacks, coupled with the arrogance of America's superpower fantasies, enabled the Defense Department to intrude into areas normally the domain of the State Department. Secretary of Defense Donald Rumsfeld's ignorant and undiplomatic references to an "Old Europe and a New Europe" when optimism about the invasion of Iraq was waning began the process of unraveling fifty years of careful and successful U.S. diplomacy to create mechanisms for European consensus. The idea of a "New Europe" and an opposing "Old Europe" was not only absurd, but it revealed the mounting desperation of the U.S. government to try to justify policies that were not substantiated with facts. The George W. Bush Administration wanted obedience, not a true process of European consensus.

The lack of perception of reality by U.S. administrations in the post-Cold War world is clear from America's view of itself on the world scene. The United States is not and has not been a superpower since the end of the Vietnam War. A superpower must possess certain attributes. These are a vast military industrial complex, a large landmass (in excess of 2 million square miles), a large and skilled population (at least 150 million people), and a coalition of allies who would be willing to act in consort with the aspiring superpower. Finally, it is absolutely essential to have a permanent nationwide military draft to maintain large standing military forces to meet any contingency. The Soviet Union, contrary to Pentagon scare tactics, never was a superpower because it did not have a credible coalition of willing partners who could be counted on to fight on Moscow's behalf. Its Warsaw Pact partners were unreliable "allies" and potential defectors to the West. The Pentagon's claims of growing Soviet threats to our security reflected not objective facts, but a need to justify the vastly inflated Department of Defense budgets for weapons programs that were important for employment in the districts of key senators and congressional representatives. Obviously, the U.S. has not had a draft since the Vietnam War and is very unlikely to reconstitute one. Since the collapse of the USSR, our partners in Europe have become much more independent and choosy about making hasty commitments to American adventures. After all, there is no military threat from Russia—and there probably never was one. No serious Soviet plans for invading Western Europe were ever found following the collapse of the Soviet Union. The former Warsaw Pact nations have confirmed the absence of any such plans.

Historically, with regard to Western Europe and America, Russia, including during the Soviet period, has not had aggressive invasion plans. Contrary to the Pentagon's misleading assertions, Russia's military planning has been and still is fundamentally defensive. With the emergence and development of the European Union, it appears that invasions of Russia from the West are very unlikely. Furthermore, it is quite unlikely that America's European allies will blindly obey Washington's calls for support unless the U.S. can make a very good case for its proposed actions.

The American reaction to the refusal of France to accept the very weak arguments that the U.S. was putting forth, at that time, for the invasion of Iraq, unmasked the arrogance, lack of sophistication, and profound ignorance of so many Americans and their government. Silly attempts to change the names of French foods and the discarding of French wines displayed the spoiled child and vengeful nature of some Americans. Many suddenly became historians and recalled the 1944 D-Day landings to free France from Nazi control and called the French ungrateful. It should be noted that the U.S. did not invade Western Europe alone. America led a coalition of nations that included the British, Canadians, Free French, Australians, Free Poles, and soldiers of many other allied countries that were against the Axis powers. It should also be noted, because it rarely is in America's highly nationalistic versions of World War II, that our greatest ally in the invasion of western Europe was the Soviet Union, which had already defeated most of Nazi Germany's best armies and, at the time of the Normandy landings, was continuing to crush most of the remaining German and other Axis allied armies. In the absence of these vast Russian military victories against the Nazis and their remaining allies, Hitler would have been able to reinforce greatly his armies in Western Europe, and a successful U.S.-led invasion of France would not have been possible in 1944. Another point to make on the American-led invasion of France was that its purpose was not just the liberation of France, but also the prevention of a Soviet occupation of Western Europe. American history books on World War II need major changes to reflect more accurately what really happened in both the European and Pacific war zones.

Those who claim that France has an obligation to support the United States because of the U.S.'s predominant role in the Normandy invasions insult the memory of those who died and those who were wounded in the invasion. Americans and their allies did not fight to free France and the rest of Western Europe from Nazi and Fascist control so that these countries would then become stooges and "yes countries" of the United States. If that were the case, the U.S. would have been no better than the USSR, which imposed strict obedience over the areas of Europe that its armies "liberated" from Nazi control. Apparently, Soviet imperialistic thinking lives on in the minds of many Americans. France and Germany, as free nations, have every right to disagree with the United States when they feel that America is not making a good case for its position on a matter in question. Free peoples not only have the right but the obligation to speak up and question any leader or any government. That was a main reason America fought to free Europe in WWII and remained on guard in Europe until internal forces brought about the end of the USSR. Americans should learn from France and Germany to question their own leaders, government officials, and the powerful lobbies that fund their election campaigns. The second Bush Administration and its backers have gotten the U.S. into two inconclusive wars in Afghanistan and Iraq that have cost many lives in both those countries as well as among the Western armed forces that have been and are participating in these military campaigns. These two wars have also radicalized many more young Moslems and aided the anti-Western movements in recruiting new members.

If American foreign policies during the previous fifty years had been free from the corrupting and self-serving interests of the money-laden lobbies, these two wars and the loss of life incurred probably could have been avoided. This would have required that the West not tread heavily in Iran on behalf of the oil industry; thus, the support for anti-Western groups would not have grown so greatly. In this scenario, there would have been no need to give Saddam Hussein weapons of mass destruction to use against Iran, because Iran would not have taken a violent turn against the U.S. and other Western countries. Also, there would have been no need to station Western troops on Saudi soil (one of Osama bin Laden's big grievances against the U.S.) during the 1991 Gulf War, because Saddam would not have been built up militarily by America, Britain, France, and Germany to the point where he felt he could settle disputes (e.g., over Kuwait) on his own terms. These mistakes—the overthrow of the 1953 Iranian government, the backing and arming of the anti-Soviet resistance in Afghanistan, the backing and heavy arming of the Saddam Hussein regime, the unnecessary and very poorly thought-out invasion of Iraq, the extreme favoritism shown toward Israel, and the familiar Western intrusiveness in economic and cultural matters—created the environment in which Moslem extremists, who normally would have been fringe players, were able to draw upon deep feelings of inadequacy, cultural and material inferiority, irrational fears, and profound historical suspicions of the West to gain large followings of young militants who saw the West as the source of the main problems in their societies. Certainly, the Americans never really knew with whom they were dealing amongst the anti-Soviet resistance fighters in Afghanistan or amongst the many warlords they encountered during the Bush Administration's first invasion of Afghanistan. The ultimate blindness was our supplying Moslem militants like Osama bin Laden and others of that type, and later, Saddam Hussein, whose plans and ambitions would lead the U.S. into two wars against Iraq. Know your enemy, but also know your "allies."

Instead of understanding the subtleties of Moslem-Western relations and the importance for Moslems of certain historical events and issues, the Middle East policies of the U.S. have been characterized by "calls for crusades," tough-guy talk, and continued subservience to the powerful lobbies that have blinded America to its true role of fostering a new world order of the rule of law and peaceful economic advances on all continents. The overwhelming power of the numerous pro-Israel lobbies and the petroleum lobby have led to the U.S. policies of unilateralism and preemptive military strikes (both discredited Israeli policies) that have now cast America in the role of a dangerous "loose cannon" bordering on being an outlaw nation. Because of its vast economic, military, cultural, and political power, the United States must move and perform like an agile and confident ballerina on the world stage so as not to seem overwhelmingly dominant. Otherwise, if the U.S. performs like the 900-pound gorilla that it has become, Washington will find few friends and plenty of opportunities to become involved in inconclusive quagmires.

The first step for the U.S. in attempting to salvage something of its moral leadership is for Washington to recognize the authority and indictments of the International Criminal Court in The Hague. This will immediately signal to the world that the leaders of the United States will be held accountable for their acts, even when in office. The neoconservative cabal that got us into Afghanistan and Iraq included President G. W. Bush and Vice President Cheney (the two presiding officials of these U.S. fiascos), Paul Wolfowitz and Richard Perle (prime architects and apologists of the current messes in Afghanistan and Iraq), and Donald Rumsfeld (the military mastermind of our quagmires in both Afghanistan and Iraq). They should not be protected by a spineless, complicit, and lobby-bought Congress that will refuse to prosecute them for foreign policy crimes (lying about having proof of the existence of weapons of mass destruction in Iraq, engaging in an unjustified preemptive war in Iraq, and continued lying about Saddam Hussein as a prime sponsor and key ally of terrorist groups). These deceptions and outright lies have needlessly caused massive destruction and a huge number of deaths and injuries in a country that did not pose a threat to the U.S. The United States can redeem itself if it takes the lead in allowing these five individuals and others to face a trial over their involvement in the planning and execution of the Iraq War. The Bush Administration must not be allowed to whitewash its tragically mistaken and deadly policies by falsely claiming to be the "crusaders of democracy" in these latest U.S. foreign policy and military debacles. Americans must end their childish and naive "fuehrer worship" of the "commander-in-chief." All commanders-in-chief must be watched and held accountable for their actions. No president should ever be above scrutiny or prosecution. Congress failed the American people in hastily going along with President George W. Bush's Iraq War. Unfortunately, calls to patriotism are frequently used to mask the lack of substance in the arguments of opportunistic political leaders.

The U.S.'s mindless policies of intensely collaborating with and arming Israel in its self-defeating attempts to suppress and brutalize the Palestinian Arabs coincides with Washington's shameful policies of actively aiding in the brutal and genocidal treatment of the Kurds by various Turkish governments. The United States completes this circle of diplomatic bankruptcy with its long-standing policies of endlessly dealing with corrupt, reactionary, and anti-democratic Arab and non-Arab Moslem regimes that cooperate with U.S. economic interests while keeping their own people suppressed and disenfranchised. The political, military, economic, and diplomatic record of America in the Middle East is appalling. It is difficult to imagine any other policies that would make the U.S. less popular in the region. The only thing that is somewhat mysterious is why it took the Arabs and their Moslem supporters so long to strike directly at the United States. It seems that the vast majority naively believed that America actually did represent all those fine values and principles that Washington claims are the essence of the U.S. The Arab hope appears to have been that America would eventually snap out of its mental paralysis and correct its shameful ways. Lamentably, even the "shock and awe" of the September 11 attacks failed to bring the United States to its senses. The unyielding grip of lobby campaign contributions has certainly been proven beyond all doubts.

It must be emphasized for *realpolitik* types that foreign policies based on our best values do not preclude "temporary alliances of convenience" with unsavory regimes. Certainly, our World War II alliance with the USSR was crucial in defeating the greater evil of Nazi Germany. But we must never forget who our "ally" is and that it is an alliance of convenience. The U.S. must not become married to these regimes and should always attempt to influence them, if necessary through inducements, to improve their human rights policies and to pressure them to moderate the sad suppression of their citizenry. If these regimes cannot make progress in these areas over a reasonable period of time (five to ten years), then the U.S. should begin to deactivate its alliance with the regime in question or America itself will become tarnished by the unacceptable and inhumane conduct of its unsavory ally. Washington's poorly thought-out adventure to remove Saddam Hussein included the terrible mistakes of disregard for our traditional allies (unilateralism), a preemptive military attack (Israeli-style), and extreme arrogance. The arrogance has been particularly evident in America's self-defeating denial of Geneva Convention protections to many prisoners that the U.S. captured. The world was stunned by the Bush-Cheney Administration's cavalier attitude toward the very serious issues of the use of torture, renditions, and not bringing prisoners to trial or to pretrial hearings.

America's lack of serious plans for administering Iraq beyond idealistic desires to turn Iraq into a democratic showplace in the Middle East revealed either naiveté or an opportunistic attempt by pro-Israeli policymakers to use the U.S. to secure the Middle East objectives of Israel in its quest to continue its military domination of the region. If the latter is true, then the enormous power of the pro-Israel lobbies has been demonstrated most convincingly and disastrously. These events in Iraq have now definitely enabled the U.S. to push Russia aside and seize the top spot as the most hated enemy of Moslems around the world. This Iraq War fiasco will be studied for many years as a prime example of political, military, and economic incompetence and systemic government failure on the part of the United States. The world is now a much more dangerous place for Americans and Westerners in general because of the brainless arrogance of the twenty-first century Bush Administration.

In spite of Washington's very poor record in the Middle East, not all is negative in the present-day American record abroad. Thankfully, a wide range of U.S. government and private American assistance programs in many foreign lands, including Islamic countries, redeem respect and honor for the United States. Those individuals who work so hard in these programs are the real American heroes that the rest of the world sees as their friends. Unfortunately, one of the tragic consequences of the self-defeating U.S. policies in the Moslem countries is that these heroes have been made into possible reprisal targets by Moslem extremists, who now view all Westerners as the enemy.

In summation, if the United States is to lead the world to a new and superior era, it will have to undergo a top-to-bottom internal political revolution that must eliminate the corrupt plutocratic financial domination of American politics by lobbies. No lobby should be in a position to "buy" or "pressure" any state or federal official. American campaigns should be restricted in terms of length. The brevity of the campaigns will reduce the circus atmosphere of elections, and those who are incumbents would not be absent from their jobs for long periods while they were campaigning. Certain media outlets will be unhappy with the reduced spending, but it is necessary to clean up our politics so America can regain its role as the great democracy and inspired leader of our times.

NOTES

1. Donald E. Queller and Thomas F. Madden, *The Fourth Crusade: The Conquest of Constantinople* (Philadelphia: University of Pennsylvania Press, 1997), 191–96. "The scale of destruction is difficult to imagine. The barbaric nature of this event is highlighted by the fact that the crusaders were destroying cultural artifacts and monuments of their own civilization."

2. Ronald Sanders, *The High Walls of Jerusalem: A History of the Balfour Declaration and the Birth of the British Mandate for Palestine* (New York: Holt, Rinehart and Winston, 1983), 409–11. "The upper ranks of Great Britain's leaders of this era contained many 'Christian Zionists,' who at best were ambivalent towards the Jews and at the same time whose ranks contained many persons eager to push as many Jews as possible out of the British Isles back into the Middle East whence they had come."

3. Ibid., 580–81.

4. Tom Segev, *One Palestine, Complete: Jews and Arabs Under the British Mandate* (New York: Metropolitan Books, 1999), 90.

5. Ibid., 377.

6. Ibid., 331.

7. Ibid., 508.

8. Walter Laqueur, *The Struggle for the Middle East: The Soviet Union in the Mediterranean, 1958–1968* (New York: Macmillan, 1969), 78–79.

9. Arthur Koestler, *Promise and Fulfillment: Palestine, 1917–49*

(London: Macmillan, 1949), 7. Koestler in the end was a supporter of the Zionist enterprise.
10. Segev, 50.
11. Ibid., 44.

FURTHER READINGS

Bodansky, Yossef. *The High Cost of Peace: How Washington's Middle East Policy Left America Vulnerable to Terrorism.* Roseville, CA: Prima Publishing, 2002. This detailed study of the many pitfalls of any peace agreement between Israel and its Arab neighbors makes clear the futility of this quest within the parameters of traditional diplomacy.

Bookbinder, Hyman, and James Abourezh. *Through Different Eyes: Two Leading Americans, a Jew and an Arab, Debate U.S. Policy in the Middle East.* Bethesda, MD: Adler & Adler, 1987. Two able spokespersons present strong arguments for their respective constituencies. The intractable nature of the Arab-Israeli conflict is made apparent in these well-reasoned presentations.

Chomsky, Noam. *9-11.* New York: Seven Stories Press, 2001. Professor Chomsky's reputation for independence and individualistic thinking is continued and strengthened in this work. His arguments on the terrorist nature of many of America's policies will inform the uninformed.

Finnie, David H. *Pioneers East.* Cambridge, MA: Harvard University Press, 1967. An interesting and informative volume on the experiences of American missionaries and travelers in the Middle East during the early and mid-nineteenth century.

Gabrieli, Francesco. *Arab Historians of the Crusades.* Los Angeles: University of California Press, 1969. A revealing and almost personal series of studies of the crusades. It is full of insights that seem lacking in Western works on this subject. All serious students of the crusades must read it.

Goodwin, Jason. *Lords of the Horizons*. New York: Henry Holt & Company, 1998. This excellent interpretive survey of Ottoman history makes clear the complex mix of cultures and peoples that composed this very eclectic empire. Those who read this book will understand modern Turkey, the Balkans, and the Near East much better.

Hourani, Albert. *A History of the Arab Peoples*. New York: MJF Books, 1991. The finest comprehensive survey of the history of the Arabs. It is a must-read for anyone who wishes to understand the Middle East.

Ingrams, Doreen. *Palestine Paper, 1917–1922*. New York: George Braziller, 1972. A detailed discussion of the meetings and conferences of these crucial years. The entangled situation in which the British found themselves during the 1920s, 1930s, and 1940s is rooted in this period.

Kent, Marian. *Oil & Empire: British Policy & Mesopotamian Oil, 1900–1920*. New York: Macmillan, 1976. Britain's obsession with the control of Middle Eastern oil supplies is clear in this study of London's imperialistic activities during the first two decades of the twentieth century.

Koestler, Arthur. *Promise and Fulfillment: Palestine, 1917–49*. London: Macmillan, 1949. Koestler was a backer of the Zionist enterprise. He also saw the injustices being planned for Palestinian Arabs.

Laqueur, Walter. *The Struggle for the Middle East: The Soviet Union in the Mediterranean, 1958–1968*. New York: Macmillan, 1969. A fine study of the less-than-admirable activities of the USSR in the Middle East during a very dangerous decade. Soviet activities did not aid world peace.

Mango, Cyril. *The Oxford History of Byzantium*. New York: Oxford University Press, 2002. One of the greatest experts on the Eastern Roman Empire illuminates many areas of its history that are so important for understanding not only Christian-Moslem relations, but also western Christian and eastern Christian relations. The physical disappearance of the empire and its replacement by the Ottoman Empire only serves to cause even more confusion and mystery in the minds of those in the West.

Palmer, Alan. *The Decline and Fall of the Ottoman Empire*. New York: Barnes & Noble, Inc., 1992. The slow but inevitable decline of the Ottoman Empire is given life and makes for enlightening reading. The roots of the political and economic problems that manifested themselves in early-twentieth century Palestine and the Middle East are made apparent in this fine study.

Queller, Donald E., and Thomas F. Madden. *The Fourth Crusade: The Conquest of Constantinople*. Philadelphia: University of Pennsylvania Press, 1997. An excellent recounting of the tragic political and economic maneuverings that led to the capture of the capital of the dying empire and the resulting horrific Western atrocities visited upon its inhabitants and their institutions. Many of the suspicions of the West that are commonly held by Orthodox Christians (including the Russians and the Ukrainians) can be understood in reading this volume.

Sanders, Ronald. *The High Walls of Jerusalem: A History of the Balfour Declaration and the Birth of the British Mandate in Palestine*. New York: Holt, Rinehart and Winston, 1983. A detailed exploration of the circumstances surrounding the Balfour Declaration and the origins of the British Mandate in Palestine. The author clearly shows the diversity of opinions that dominated the discussions on Palestine.

Segev, Tom. *One Palestine, Complete: Jews and Arabs Under the British Mandate.* New York: Metropolitan Books, 1999.This is the best recent study of the British Mandate period. The good, the bad, and everything in between is laid out for fair examination. I benefited from this work and advise all who are interested in the Middle East to read it.

Silberman, Neil Asher. *Digging for God and Country: Exploration, Archeology, and the Secret Struggle for the Holy Land, 1799–1917*. New York: Alfred A. Knopf, 1982. This study uncovers a heady mix of idealism, religious mysticism, political intrigue, economic maneuvering, and ever-present imperial ambitions in what was to become the seething cauldron of

the early-twentieth century Middle East.
Stivers, William. *Supremacy and Oil: Iraq, Turkey, and the Anglo-American World Order, 1918–1930.* Ithaca, NY: Cornell University Press, 1982. This work clearly shows how the U.S. tried to push its commercial agenda throughout this twelve year-period. British and American diplomatic and economic issues with Iraq, Turkey, and the Arabs are explored.
Zepezauer, Mark. *Boomerang!: How Our Covert Wars Have Created Enemies Throughout the Middle East and Brought Terror to America*. Monroe, ME: Common Courage Press, 2003. This is an exposé of the self-destructive pattern of American foreign policies in the Middle East and other parts of the world. It would be a very good idea for U.S. leaders to read this book instead of trying to base American foreign policies in the Middle East on biblical insights and superpower fantasies.

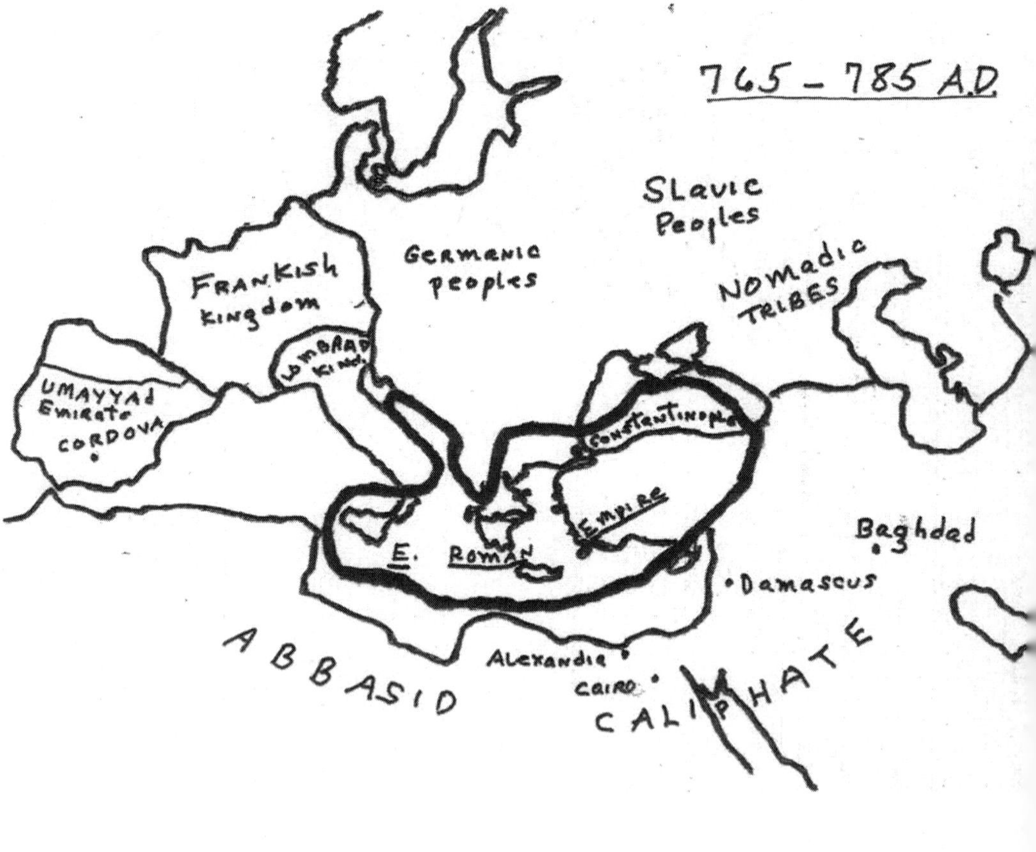
765 – 785 A.D.
Slavic Peoples
Germanic peoples
FRANKISH kingdom
NOMADIC TRIBES
UMAYYAD Emirate
CORDOVA
Constantinople
E. ROMAN Empire
Baghdad
Damascus
Alexandie
CAIRO
ABBASID
CALIPHATE

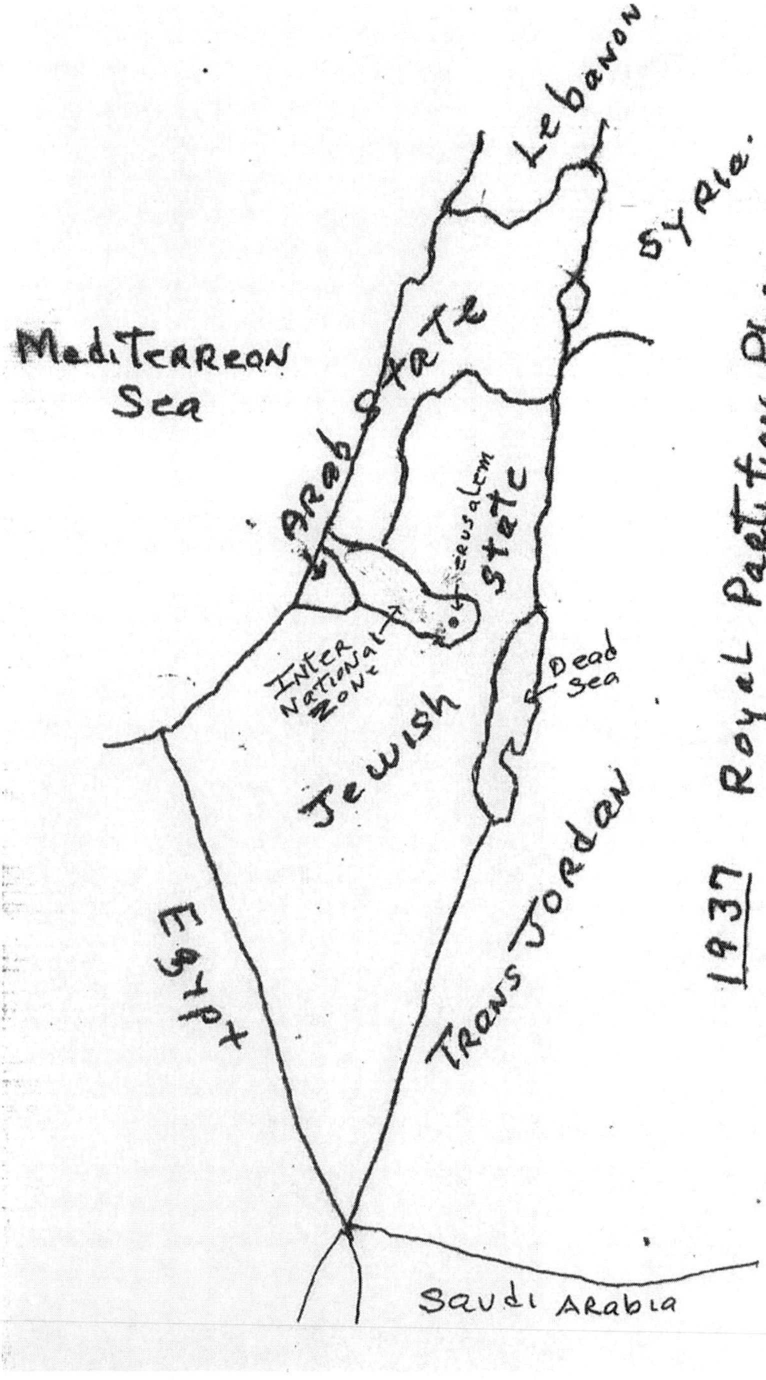

1937 Royal Partition Plan

2009
Beirut
Lebanon
Damascus
Syria
Tel Aviv
Israel
West Bank
Jerusalem
Amman
Dead Sea
Gaza Strip
Jordan
Egypt
Saudi Arabia

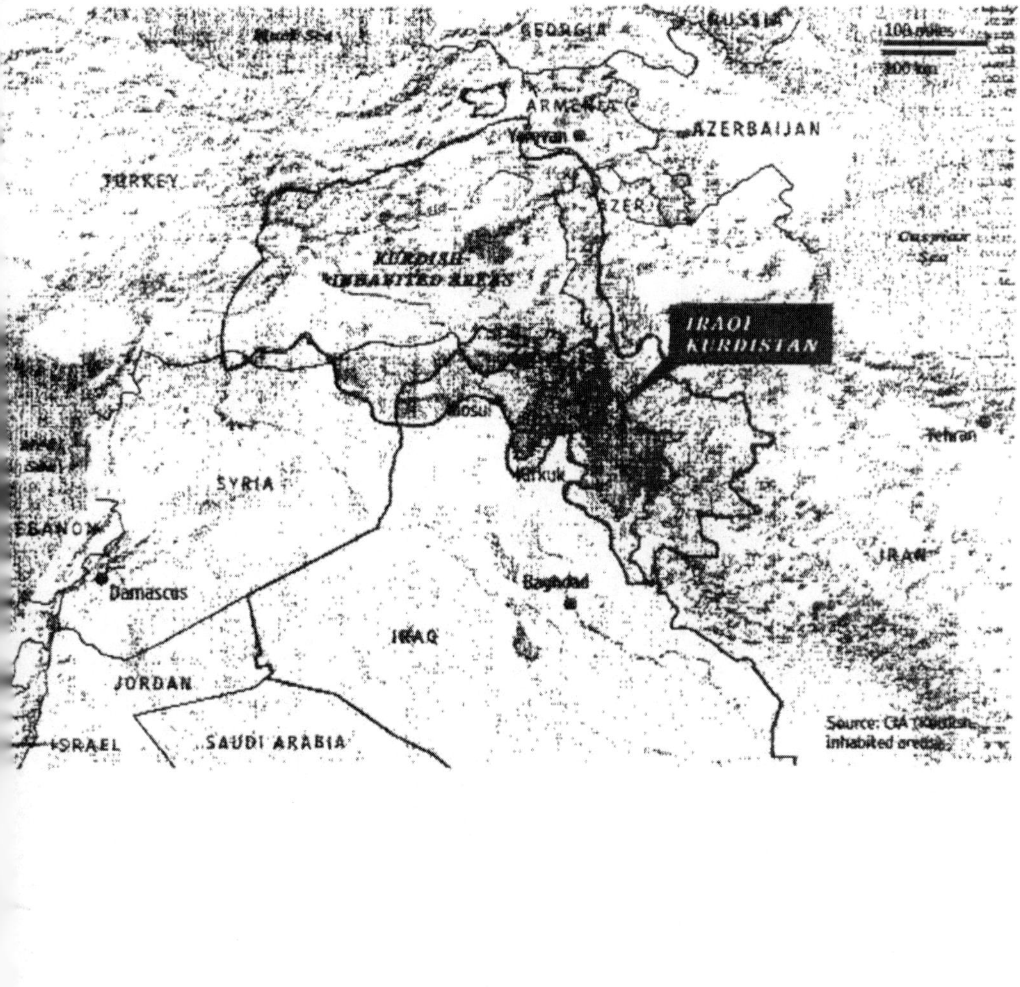
GEORGIA
ARMENIA
AZERBAIJAN
TURKEY
KURDISH-INHABITED AREAS
IRAQI KURDISTAN
SYRIA
Damascus
Baghdad
IRAQ
IRAN
Tehran
JORDAN
ISRAEL
SAUDI ARABIA